WEBSTERS
of
LUCERNE

Kay Black

ISBN 979-8-88751-153-5 (paperback)
ISBN 979-8-88751-154-2 (digital)

Copyright © 2023 by Kay Black

All rights reserved. No part of this publication may be reproduced, distributed, or transmitted in any form or by any means, including photocopying, recording, or other electronic or mechanical methods without the prior written permission of the publisher. For permission requests, solicit the publisher via the address below.

Christian Faith Publishing
832 Park Avenue
Meadville, PA 16335
www.christianfaithpublishing.com

Printed in the United States of America

This book is dedicated to the men and boys who have worked deep in the Earth to provide comfort to all mankind. To the Andrews, Walters, and Henrys, we owe you our eternal gratitude. Many are still down there, buried beneath rubble, forever entombed. God rest their souls!

COAL

By definition, coal is a hard black mineral burned as fuel and is vital to many industries. Coal is formed from compressing the remains of tropical and subtropical plants. Coal occurs in all continents, even Antarctica. The process begins when plant debris accumulates in swamps, decomposes, and forms peat. When buried beneath the weight of water or land subsidence, the peat is transformed under high temperature into coal. The greater the pressure, the harder the coal. Coals are classified or ranked according to their fixed-carbon content, which increases progressively as they are formed. The main types of coal are the following:[1]

- Lignite or brown coal—weathers quickly, may ignite spontaneously, has a low caloric value, and is mostly used in Germany and Australia
- Subbituminous—mainly used in generating stations
- Bituminous—the most commonly used in generating stations and for home use and is converted into coke
- Anthracite—a lustrous coal that burns slowly and efficiently and is preferred for domestic fuel

Coal has a long history of use, as early as 2 BC, and was known in China and the Roman Empire around the time of Christ. Coal was mined throughout Europe and American Indians by the thirteenth century AD.

---

[1] The Concord Desk Encyclopedia, 1982.

The first commercial coal mine in the US was in Richmond, Virginia, which opened in 1745, and anthracite was mined in Pennsylvania by 1790. A huge and increasing demand for coal was brought about during the industrial revolution. Other fuels such as oil and gas replaced coal in the twentieth century. The annual production of coal yields approximately 3 billion tons, 500 million of the total coming from the US. Reserves from all over the world are estimated at 7 trillion tons. At the present rate of use, there is enough to meet the demand for several centuries.

I would venture to say that nearly every human living in a developed country on Earth is affected by the mining and use of coal—from cooking, heating homes, and generating electricity to powering steam trains, manufacturing steel for our automobiles, powering farm machinery, and fueling trucks to transport the merchandise we purchase at stores built with steel girders. The list is too long to include every way our lives depend on coal.

When a coal company's geologists found an abundance of coal, they would build entire towns. Sears, Roebuck and Co. houses were erected, and the miners paid through installment plans to purchase them. Company doctors were brought in. General stores were owned by the coal company and were where miners spent all the money they earned and then some. As Tennessee Ernie Ford sang, "I owe my soul to the company store." The town's utilities were established, and schools built for the many children. Churches were established for those who believed, and most did since prayer was all they had to give them faith that their men and boys would walk out of the mines at quitting time.

My parents bought one of these mining-town houses, tore it down, and rebuilt it on a plot of land they purchased. The house had a living room, a kitchen, one bedroom, and a porch. The "facilities" were in the basement. My parents enclosed the porch to create another bedroom. The house was heated by coal. I was born in that house and lived there until age ten when we moved. I dreaded the coal delivery day; it was when a fine black layer of dust settled over the house's interior. Everything had to be cleaned. Lace curtains were taken down, washed, and stretched on pin frames. The wallpaper was cleaned with a product similar to Silly Putty. However, coal delivery day allowed a welcome sound to wake me on winter mornings when my dad would go to the huge furnace in the basement and shake down ashes from the firebox, which had been banked overnight. I knew the house would be warm when I crawled out of bed. (My older sister married and lived in the same house until she passed. They have built an addition and converted it to an oil furnace.)

Although I was young, I helped with removing the ashes then emptying them onto the driveway to give traction for car tires over compacted snow. I learned to ride a bike on that driveway and the red-dog road in front of our house. Red dog is what was left after coal was burned to make coke. I was careful not to fall since that red dog would really bite into any exposed skin. The smoke from the coke ovens was a permanent fixture in the town of Ernest, not far from my childhood home.

What follows is a story about one fictional family in a former mining town in southwestern Pennsylvania. This could have been anyone, but this is the Webster family's story.

PART 1

EARLY SPRING 2005–JUNE 2015

1

EMMA MAE SMITH WEBSTER

With one last gasp for air, Walter shuddered and died. A simple cold took his ability to breathe. His struggle was over. Emma's struggle would continue since she knew her life was going to change dramatically now that she didn't have her husband to care for and their children were raised and on their own. Emma quickly changed from her night clothes.

Her first call was Betsy, from Visiting Nurse Association, who came daily to check on Walter and administer his medical needs. When Emma heard Betsy's hello, "Betsy, he is gone," was all she said before breaking down into sobs.

"I'll be right there, Emma." Betsy arrived scant minutes later, dressed in proper uniform as always although it was early morning. She checked for a pulse and normal responses and established time of death. "You are a brave woman, Emma. Not many women would have attended Walter as well as you have over the years. I have seen women crack under these circumstances."

"He was my husband. I meant those vows all those years ago." Emma accepted a hug from Betsy before calling their friend, Alvin Wolfe, at the local mortuary.

Nora Simpson, Emma's best friend and across-the-road neighbor, came bustling in, wearing an apron over her housedress and still in bedroom slippers, as soon as she saw Wolfe Funeral Home's hearse in the driveway. "Emma Mae, now you sit down and let me get you a cup of tea." Nora tried to distract Emma, but they watched from the living room as Alvin Wolfe removed Walter's lifeless body from the dining room, which had been converted to a bedroom for the duration of Walter's final months of illness. Stairs were such a chore for Walter, causing him to struggle to breathe as his lungs deteriorated from black lung contracted while working in the coal mine. The upstairs rooms, as well as the addition, were closed off to conserve heat and reduce Emma's workload.

Nora notified the church's Ladies Society and made some official calls. However, Emma composed herself enough to make calls to notify their three children. Emma reached daughter Carol at her home in Vienna, Virginia.

"I promise I'll be back home to Lucerne as soon as I finish my writing deadline. I will collect homework assignments for Susie and Roberta for the time they will miss school," Carol responded, barely able to speak.

Emma left a voice mail message for son Robert. "Robbie, this is your mother. Give me a call as soon as you get this message." His job as an airline pilot could have him anywhere in the world. She would have to wait until he called back, and who knew when that would be. She wanted to tell him in person, not just leave a message on his answering machine telling him his dad died.

Next, she called the Red Cross, giving them Jimbo's name, rating, and name of the ship he served on in the U.S. Navy. A Mr. Reynolds called back two hours later with the news, "AJ James A. Webster's ship is out to sea on maneuvers. Due to the classified mission, they are unreachable for anything other than national emergencies." He was full of apologies, but that didn't help much.

When she realized she didn't have any more pressing matters, she sent Nora back home by saying, "There are times one just needs to be alone to figure things out." Too upset to sit down, she wandered through their home, wondering how she was going to go on. For the last six months, she spent every day and night taking care of Walter. She slept on a recliner next to his rented hospital bed. She had not been upstairs to their bedroom for weeks. She slowly climbed the stairs to look for burial clothes for Walter and to get out her good black dress to check if it still fit. She feared she may have lost too much weight while attending to Walter's needs and neglecting her own. Meals were cold and unappetizing by the time she finished feeding him, and she lost her appetite due to fatigue of staying up half the night listening to his labored breathing.

While sorting through their closet, she reminisced about meeting Walter, becoming good friends in seventh grade when Tommy Thrower, an upperclassman was tormenting her, making inappropriate advances. Walter intervened, telling the bully he would have to answer to him if there were any further inappropriate behavior. Due to Walter's healthy size, there would be no more problems with Tommy or anyone else after word spread Walter Webster was protecting Emma Mae Smith. They became friends that turned into going steady, then dating when she was old enough.

Walter quit school when he turned sixteen to work in the coal mine with his grandfather, father, and uncles. As soon as Walter got his driver's license, he was assigned to the motor, a small train going in and out of the mine, carrying miners or loads of coal. A canary was transported into the mine to detect gases that could ignite if a metal shovel hitting rock caused a spark. If the canary died, miners were evacuated. Gas explosions caused cave-ins, which suffocated and trapped miners, sometimes burying them alive. He didn't like taking that poor canary in there every day with the men. The feathers would be bright yellow in the morning but black with coal dust when quitting-time whistle blew. Coal dust coated everyone and everything, got into their food, up their noses, and down their throats into their lungs. Miners didn't live long, and owners of mines didn't seem to care.

She and Walter remained sweethearts after he left school, and they married soon after Emma's high school graduation. She moved into the Webster homestead to take care of her father-in-law in declining health from black lung. There were so many rooms to clean and laundry to do, and she helped her mother-in-law look after Walter's younger siblings. One by one, as each sibling left home for schooling or jobs, the workload grew easier.

For a few years, Emma also worked at the local bank while keeping their home running as smoothly as possible. After their own children were born, she quit her day job and started cleaning offices in the BNP Coal Company office at night when Walter was at home with the children. She needed to work since every penny she earned counted. They signed for groceries and nearly everything else they needed at The Company Store. On payday, almost nothing was left after the Company Store bill was paid, if two paychecks covered the whole bill. For any serious shopping, which didn't happen often since no one had extra money, town residents would have to drive to Greensburg or Indiana.

The town of Lucerne was nice enough, if it could be called a town. There wasn't much of a business district except for the post office, The Company Store, Wolfe's Funeral Home, the Mine Office (which closed when the mine was shut down), Randall Block's law office, and ever-present tavern where any leftover money was spent on booze. The large school educated K-12 grades all in one building. Three churches were grouped together on the edge of town: Presbyterian, Lutheran, and Catholic.

The narrow two-story houses, built by the coal company, were all the same, with the only variables being an occasional decorative porch railing, a fence to contain dogs and kids, unless someone with some decorating sense and a couple gallons of paint made a difference. The lawns were of poor soil coated with coal dust settled out of smoke-filled air. Some families, with a knack for gardening, grew a small plot of vegetables such as the always-popular cabbage, carrots, lettuce, and radishes. If a family had more land than the standard seventy-five-by-one-hundred-foot town lot, potatoes were planted. Potatoes cooked in many different ways were a mainstay in the local diet.

The countryside was peaceful after all the mining shut down, with beautiful scenery, green hills, and lush valleys. The next county had some trouble with another coal company clear-cutting trees and pushing them into the valleys, blocking streams, killing wildlife, and choking life out of the region. Hills were being stripped down to reach coal veins near the surface. When coal was depleted, land was left barren, boulder strewn, and with rocky soil unable to grow even a lowly weed. Attempts to reforest failed since the topsoil was gone, pushed into streams.

With deep mining, there were occasional problems with cave-ins causing water wells to fail or pipes from wells to separate from houses. So far, God blessed the Websters with good luck. Their property was on the western side of town away from coal dust, where green pastures fed beef cattle and dairy cows. Where land was too steep, sheep grazed then provided wool as a cash crop, and goats kept them in milk while keeping fields neatly trimmed. Those steep hills hid the ugliness of underground mines.

Emma Mae grew up used to hard work on her family's farm north of town. Her father gave up mining when his older brother, Robert, died in a cave-in. Although farmwork was just as hard with many hazards, he wanted to provide a safe environment for his growing family plus Robert's widow and two sons. He would do anything to keep his sons and nephews out of mining.

Emma worked as hard as her two older brothers. She drove tractor, loaded hay bales onto a wagon, and then unloaded the wagon onto a conveyor taking bales into the barn's loft where her brothers stacked them. She got up at five thirty and helped with the milking before going to school or church, with her hair smelling like barn in spite of showering.

She wasn't the only one in this half-farming, half-mining community. She learned to card and spin wool from sheep she raised for 4-H, all while learning the woman's role in cooking huge meals at threshing time, making homemade lye and goat-milk soap, in addition to supporting and assisting the men. She was denied any advanced schooling beyond a high school diploma, although her two brothers were encouraged to go to college. Her brother, Edward, became a civil engineer and moved to Ohio. Brother John became a forest ranger and worked in Yellowstone National Park, far away from the coal mines they hated.

As she walked through the house, she noted how Walter's father's woodworking talent was evident everywhere in this huge house. Stair railings were hand carved by Pap Webster from their own trees. He decorated most rooms with crown molding and handmade furniture. The floors were wide-plank style, handlaid by Pap and his three boys, all gone now to their heavenly reward. The eaves and porches were decorated with gingerbread trim. Walter loved this house where he and his siblings grew up. Even though it was too big and too ornate for such simple folk, he would not consider living anywhere else. They closed off the large addition, which was built to house an expanding family, making do with the original house.

They lived comfortably enough for many years. Then Walter started coughing, the first sign of black lung. She didn't know how much longer he would be able to work. At her cleaning job at BNP Coal Company's office, she paid attention when she overheard conversations about avoiding lawsuits and saw interoffice memos in wastebaskets she emptied that were not in favor of miners. There was no comfort in knowing everyone in town was affected by coal mining. It was a rare family who didn't have at least one person working in the mines. She became a major caretaker as her parents aged and died. Soon after their parents were gone, Walter got too sick to work. They got in touch with their friend and attorney, Randall Block, and he took their case to court.

Emma's mind was whirling with memories as she went through the day trying to straighten up the house from long months of neglect. She made lists of things to do before family came. Walter was gone, and she felt her life was flashing before her like an old newsreel. She relived her childhood, her teenage years, and the early years with Walter as one of her best friends, besides Nora whom she also got to know in seventh grade. She recalled the births of her babies, even the one she only knew a few days. Her working life was best left alone, but she remembered avoiding a few men who might be working late. They kept liquor in their desk drawers and lost some of their manners if given half a chance.

Poignantly, her thoughts lingered on Walter's sweetness as his black lung sapped his energy. After he stopped working, he was able to putter around in his woodshop, and he went fishing, sometimes taking her along to row the boat. He walked to the store to spend some time visiting with friends before walking back home to take a nap before supper. As he got worse, he stayed in the house more, talking less to save his breath.

But every now and then, they would sit and chat quietly. One or the other would start by saying, "Do you remember…" and conversations took off from those simple words: "Do you remember when we went ice-skating on Uncle Andy's pond? We made hot chocolate after"; "Do you remember going to the drive in? Do you remember any of the movies we saw?"; "Do you remember building a snow lady instead of a snowman? She was a purty thing, wasn't she?"

Fond memories would be their entertainment for a while. They enjoyed thinking about and remembering good times. They brought up folks they used to know, some long gone to their heavenly reward. "Do you know where Helen is since Michael passed?" Some moved away to be with children who moved to greener pastures, better jobs, less pollution. "Do you remember Jim and Martha? Where did they move? Did we get a Christmas card last year?" However, it was fun remembering youthful behavior before the act of living and breathing became a chore. They used to wonder if they would survive into the new century, which was already five years old.

Having found Walter's suit, a shirt, and a tie he only wore for holiday church services, she came back to the present day when she went to the kitchen to fix a simple meal to carry into the living room to eat in front of the TV. Out of habit and pure exhaustion of keeping vigil, she fell asleep in a well-worn recliner.

She woke up in the middle of the night, turned off the TV infomercial, stretched, and slowly walked once more through the house, touching items here and there—gifts from Walter or treasures from her parents' home sold long ago. She again admired the house's beauty. She lingered for a while at the closed door of the library. This room, however, wasn't intended to be a library. She and Walter fixed this room as a nursery early in their marriage for their firstborn. After their tiny baby girl was born prematurely, they struggled, knowing she would never leave the hospital to occupy this room all decorated with bunnies.

Prayers for the tiny infant to survive went unanswered. They named her Alice Faye just hours before she passed in Emma's arms. The emptiness never left her heart, although her arms were filled a year later when Robbie was born. Losing that tiny baby girl before she had a chance to really live left unspeakable grief. She could never bring herself to share that grief with any of the rest of the family. Carol wasn't told she could have had a big sister. Losing Walter was tough, but he at least had a chance to have a life.

Although that was many years ago, Emma felt tears forming and quickly swept them away with her fingertips and could not bring herself to go into the library room. Walter used to find comfort to go in there to read, or listen to his favorite radio programs while he was still able to climb the stairs. Emma kept her favorite books in their bedroom or on bookcases next to the downstairs fireplace. She momentarily touched the doorknob but turned and slowly walked away.

Emma ended her middle-of-night walk in the big bedroom she shared with Walter for most of her adult life. Whatever would she do, rambling around in this house alone? Everyone else was gone! She was entering a strange new chapter of her life. At sixty-nine, she was a widow. She sat down at her desk, pulled a legal pad from a drawer, and made a list of things she always wanted to do. Their animals were a thing of the past. Other than maintaining house and property, with land already leased out to farmers, she was free of responsibility for the first time in her life. A pattern began to emerge, and she developed a plan for her future.

She knew the coal industry was dying with more and more companies filing Chapter 11 bankruptcy. At one point in 1923, there were 863,000 miners in this country alone, currently down to fifty thousand. The state of Pennsylvania, where she and Walter lived, worked, and raised their family, ranked fourth in production, with softer bituminous in the western part of the state and harder anthracite in the east.

The steel mills around Pittsburgh were shifting to gas-fired furnaces, reducing demand for coal, which also had an effect of less polluted air. Homeowners were converting from coal furnaces to natural gas or oil. This all fit into her five-to-ten-year plan to provide better lives for their children and the town of Lucerne. She stretched out on their bed where she fell into a deep sleep, waking when the phone began to ring.

2

LIFE GOES ON

Following her morning routine, she spent most of her time on the phone with sympathy callers. "Thank you for calling. Yes, Walter was a good man, a good provider. I will let you know when funeral arrangements are complete," she said over and over. She had so many good friends in this community. Church Society Ladies were already starting to bring food. Nora came over to help, but everyone wanted to see or talk to her. "Nora, dear, would you mind taking Walter's layout clothing to Alvin Wolfe?" Although Nora was a dear friend, there were times a person had to face the day one minute at a time. Emma was finding strength to do just that.

Carol called from Dulles airport where she told her mother she, Roberta, and Susie were boarding a plane after getting a "family emergency rate." Robbie called to say he was granted emergency time off and would arrive tomorrow as soon as he got back from San Francisco.

Relief came midafternoon when Alvin Wolfe called to say he was ready for her to come for her private viewing. Walter insisted on preplanning everything so no decisions needed to be made. Even after death, as he did as long as his health allowed, he was taking care of her. She uttered a "Thank you, Walter," before getting in her gold-colored Chevy Nova to drive the short distance. Walking wasn't an option today. Her knees were a little shaky and weakened with her feeling of grief.

Alvin greeted her and then left her alone for her private viewing. She was almost glad for one last time alone with Walter to tell him about her plan developed while awake in the wee hours of the morning. Money he received in the settlement against the coal company for his black lung disease would be used to better the community they both loved. The house was a different matter. However, there was no hurry to make any decisions. She wouldn't make major changes in her life until she knew her thinking was not being governed or clouded by grief.

After quietly telling Walter of her plan, making her ideas a reality to her own ears, she went home and called Nora to say she could use some help. They opened all the doors on the second floor, starting to prepare for arriving family. They would leave the addition closed off. There wasn't time to do much more than air out rooms, put clean linens on beds, fresh towels in bathrooms, dust furniture, vacuum, and get in a few groceries to feed the family. Donated casseroles would be a big help, but Carol's teenage daughters and Robbie would want more.

The van from Clark's Medical Supply came and removed the hospital bed to restore the dining room to its intended purpose. Nora's husband, Jake, helped move furniture around, hosed winter grime off porches, washed the old Nova and had it serviced. Walter wouldn't want her to be ashamed of it during the procession from Wolfe's Funeral Home to the church cemetery where his parents, one brother, and the rest of his ancestors were interred, including little Alice Faye.

Carol and her girls arrived late that evening after Jake picked them up at the airport. "Oh, Ma, I'm so sorry I couldn't get here before Dad died. I wanted to, you know? I just didn't want to take the girls out of school, and my jobs keep me busy. Since spring break is next week, I can stay awhile. Let me know how I can help while I'm here."

Emma could only nod and say, "Sure, I understand." Emma hugged them all and made hot chocolate, warming them from an early-spring chill in the air. Carol settled into her childhood room, and the girls settled into Jimbo's since he wouldn't be coming home any time soon. After Emma gave Carol details of her father's passing and outlined simple arrangements, they had an hour or two of chatting, mostly about Carol's jobs and teenagers' school activities. Emma decided to keep her own plans for the future to herself.

Robbie arrived early the next day and took over a lot of Emma and Carol's greeting duties, acting as man of the house. Always good to have a man around, and Robbie was a take-charge kind of man. However, men want to do everything their way, which sometimes was a bit contentious. "Ma, could I ask you to please not call me Robbie? Rob or Robert, please."

"Oh all right. But don't get upset if I slip up. I know you are a big important captain, but you'll always be my little boy," as she reached up and patted his cheek.

Emma went through the ritual of receiving friends, standing by Walter's coffin for two exhausting days of visitation and nearly being overcome with grief and nauseating smell of banks of flowers from so many people who knew and loved him. She just wanted the ordeal to be over. She made a vow to arrange her own funeral to be less taxing to her family. She would add that to her list to talk about when she saw Randall as soon as he returned from wherever he was this week.

Just days after the funeral was over, the women were almost relieved when Rob left to resume his flight schedule. Carol helped Emma go through her dad's clothing and pack some items in boxes to donate to Goodwill. However, Emma wasn't ready to release everything. Carol understood as she went through this procedure when she was widowed many years ago. When school was about to start again, Carol and her daughters went home with a promise to her mother she would return soon.

3

EMMA'S PLAN

With the funeral over and family back in their own homes living their own lives, Emma called her family attorney. "Randall, do you have time to chat today? There is no hurry. However, I have been thinking of a way to help Lucerne."

"Sure, Miz Webster. How about 2 o'clock? I'd like to help any way I can. You and Walter were substitute parents to me after my folks died."

Promptly at 2 o'clock, Mamie, Randall's secretary, ushered Emma into his office, offering to take notes. Emma politely said, "Thank you, my dear. That won't be necessary at this time." Mamie closed the door as she went back to her desk in her cramped outer office.

Randall greeted Emma warmly. "I am so sorry for being in Kentucky for a trial the previous weeks and unable to pay respects. You know I thought the world of Walter. He was a good man and will be missed."

Emma began her rehearsed speech, "Yes. Thank you, Randall. I know you are a busy man, and I understand why you couldn't be here. You have to take care of business first. I appreciate all you have done for me during Walter's illness and Jimbo being away. You have no idea how much I admire you and want to acknowledge how eloquent you were in your case against Walter's employer, BNP Coal Company. The monetary award was quite unexpected and has been invested in secured accounts. Now, with Walter gone, I have all this extra time on my hands. I want to do something for Lucerne with the awarded funds. With the mines closed and jobs lost, people are moving away. I heard property is selling at rock-bottom prices. I have a plan to invest in this town."

She saw Randall's eyebrows rise with a quizzical look. Going on, "I am sure you are wondering how I am going to do that. Here is my plan. I want to buy some choice properties and hire someone to do some remodeling and then advertise to new businesses to bring new life to town. We have lush valleys and mountain views. We can make something special out of this stagnant town. Will you help me? Oh, and I don't want people to know who is doing this."

Randall Block took a moment to absorb the intensity in Miz Webster's pale-blue eyes and steepled his fingers in front of him as he pondered her words. She sat on the edge of her chair with her petite frame dressed in her good black dress, sensible pumps, gray hair neatly styled in an out-of-date page boy, just a touch of rouge on her cheeks, and a hint of some lipstick. She looked more rested and healthier than he had seen her for several years, especially since Walter took ill.

Taking care of Walter sapped her energy. With her forthright manner, he had no doubt she believed in her plan. After a period of silent thought, he responded, "Well now, let's see. I think we need to take our time and do this right. For protection, let's get you set up with a corporation. Do you want to hire a manager? Or do you want to do the work yourself?"

"If you will help, I'd rather do the managing on my own. The fewer people who know what I am doing would be better, don't you think? Jimbo's Navy enlistment is complete in about six months. I would need to have a little space for an office away from the house if he comes back home to live."

Randall agreed with her thinking. "The adult education department at the school has courses you can take. Go to see Mr. Derickson to register. I will help get you started. I will inquire and tell the landlord I need some extra space. There is a small vacant office on the second floor of this building. I am sure my landlord would give me a good price. That will protect your identity. You need to give me a name for your corporation, and we can get started immediately."

"Since I am doing this for my children and their children and so forth, let me think on a name and get back to you in a day or two. Meanwhile, I need a realtor you know can be discreet. I have been thinking about and planning this for several weeks now. I'd like to get started as soon as possible. I have too much time on my hands."

Randall stood as Emma rose from her chair. "Yes, ma'am. I'll get started on this right away. I recommend Paul Arnold as your realtor. I'll call him and give him a heads-up."

With that, Emma excused herself, exchanging pleasantries with Mamie as she left Randall's office with her head held high and her heels clicking on the linoleum floor. Emma felt satisfied with the progress she made and their agreement. She drove to Greensburg to Best Buy, and a nice salesman helped her pick out a laptop, printer, mouse, set up an internet connection, and in-house classes to learn how to use it all. She went to see her friend Ralph Derickson in the school office in Lucerne and signed up for some adult courses Randall suggested. She went home and cleared space on her desk, where she kept all the family receipts and books to set up the computer following all detailed notes she took while listening to the salesman. "That wasn't so difficult," she said to no one in particular. She felt she would be doing more and more talking to herself in the future.

Emma called Randall two days later and said, "I have figured out a name for my corporation. What do you think of Jaroc Enterprises Inc.? I took the first few letters of the names of my children. I am doing this for them, after all."

"You have a unique name. However, I will still have to check to see if someone else is using it. I will get paperwork ready for you to sign and will call and let you know when you can come in to finalize. I have been thinking of how to make this happen, and I will be pleased and proud to help."

Emma was glad to have the support of this young man whom she had known since he and Carol were an item many years before. She once hoped they would get over their spat. They may have if Robbie hadn't been so hurt by Randall's winning a scholarship they both wanted. Robbie kept the feud going between him and Randall. Robbie enlisted in the Air Force after graduation since airplanes always intrigued him. He did well and was now a commercial pilot flying for United Airlines. Then, Carol fell for the lies of that no-good traveling salesman and moved away, Emma surmised, just to get out of town and away from the bickering. So it all turned out for the better. She could only hope Jimbo found himself in the Navy.

4

HOMECOMING FOR JAMES ALAN "JIMBO" WEBSTER

Six months later, Jimbo was back from his maneuvers, discharged from the U. S. Navy, and back in Lucerne. He soon was feeling lost. His school friends were married and having families or moved to other places with more opportunities to make a living. Some were in service to the country as he had been.

He told Ma he would only be staying for a short time. However, living at home was easy. He tried several jobs, none holding his interest for more than a few months. Before he went to the Navy, he delivered coal until the company closed the mine. Remembering that time, he eliminated becoming an over-the-road truck driver since it was not as exciting as he thought it might be—just lots of boring hours on monotonous highways. He was an aircraft mechanic in the Navy. But he didn't feel like taking tests to do the same work in civilian life, and there wasn't a close airport.

He finally took a job at The Company Store where he stocked shelves and helped with sales when Mr. Krause needed a break. Jimbo liked working with his hands, and he helped customers on evenings and weekends to install items they bought in the store. The job paid for his beer, cigarettes, plus groceries now and then to make it up to Ma for his being such a pain in the rump.

She didn't like his drinking and smoking. To please her, he put up with going outside to smoke. He stopped for a drink or two at the local tavern before going home and bought a miniature refrigerator for his bedroom to keep his drinking to himself.

Also on his days off from the store, he managed to bring his old Bronco back to life after it sat idle for four years while he was in the Navy. He needed wheels to get around. Ma's old Chevy Nova wasn't his style. He overhauled the Bronco's engine, then painted it navy blue and installed new gold seat covers. He tried to keep Ma's Nova going, but one day, she came home with a brand-new Ford Fusion. He guessed Dad must have had some insurance money.

Goodness knows she did enough running around. If she wasn't going to some church meeting with the ladies, she was getting her hair done or going to lunch with her friends. Who knew what she did with all her time? She kept the house neat and clean, a little too neat and clean for Jimbo. Meals were ready when he got home from work, and laundry was done every Monday. That was all he knew or cared about.

Missing being able to talk to his dad, he felt better while cleaning and storing all the fishing gear in the back garage or he would think about all the good times they used to have. Jimbo used to look up to his big brother and his sister. But lately, his mother's pious attitude and Robbie's condescending way of talking to him and Carol's bossiness was all getting to him, like a burr under his saddle. He was glad they lived far enough away he didn't have to put up with them on a constant basis. He could pretend to be "little brother" for a weekend now and then.

On Sunday mornings, instead of going to church with Ma like she always nagged him about, he might go out to the lake to meet his spiritual needs. He would rent a canoe and just paddle around aimlessly, sometimes with a fishing line over the stern and a six-pack of Yuengling in a cooler. Being in nature away from crowds and watching eagles perched in tops of pine trees or soaring overhead was enough proof of a supreme being, not sure he bought into all the church's teachings.

He was seeing some new buildings going up around town and considered getting a job as a carpenter. However, Mr. Krause was getting up in years. He didn't want to leave him in a lurch. He was doing okay. No use upsetting the apple cart.

5

SETBACK

Jimbo had been home about a year, and Emma was well on her way to helping the town recover. She already owned six pieces of property with Paul Arnold's help when she realized she wasn't feeling quite up to par. Just tired, but that could be a warning. She was working hard overseeing some remodeling under the guise of being curious. Sid Freeling, a contractor and close friend, did the actual work. She also realized nearly three years had passed since her last medical checkup, so she went through routine screenings and exams.

When Dr. Lawrence's nurse called her to have her mammogram repeated, she wasn't surprised. There was breast cancer in her family, and she chided herself for not being more vigilant of her own health while looking after Walter. Although she kept her weight down, she was still in a high-risk category. With the results of the second mammogram showing a suspicious area, she scheduled an ultrasound then a needle biopsy as requested.

"Miz Webster, we need to make a few decisions." Her doctor was gentle yet firm with her. "I know you spent a lot of time taking care of your husband. Now it is time to take care of you. Research has come a long way in the treatment protocol. You have many options today. The internet is full of information. Some of it is good, some misleading. Go to the American Cancer Society website, then click on breast cancer. We have a little time, but don't wait long. Make a follow-up appointment for next week at the latest." He outlined what she could expect.

Emma did some research on her own, unable to sleep much that night. Two days later, she arrived at a decision. Calling her doctor, she said, "I'm ready to give you my answer. I think I will go with the lumpectomy you described. If this were your wife or mother, what you would advise them to do?"

"I think you made a good choice. We will plan, of course, to follow up with radiation treatments just to be sure. We will do a sentinel-node biopsy during surgery to test your lymph nodes under your arm to determine if the cancer has spread. If it has, then we may need to add a round of chemotherapy. We can make further decisions postsurgery. How soon can we get you onto the surgery schedule? Since you will be under anesthesia, you need someone to drive you."

"Let's get this over with," she answered. "My son is home from his military service to drive me."

"You will be in and out the same day. The anesthesia won't last long. There will be minor discomfort for a few days, but you will be able to resume normal activities immediately as you feel up to it. You would be wise to add a short rest during the day. Put your feet up and let your body work on healing. Radiation treatments won't start until your incision is completely healed."

Emma really downplayed to Jimbo the seriousness of her procedure. He drove her to the hospital in the early morning and went to work as usual. She called him later in the afternoon when she was ready to go home. He drove her home and went back to work. She didn't feel bad. The small patches on the incision sites were well hidden under her loose-fitting clothing she was advised to wear. She placed one of her precooked casseroles in the oven for their dinner and took a nap.

Jimbo came home from work, ate, and went to the garage to work on his Bronco until nearly bedtime. While Jimbo dozed in a recliner, she sat quietly watching *Desperate Housewives* until they went their separate ways at ten.

After a month, Emma fit her trips to the hospital for radiation treatments into her normal routine. She knew any modesty she had left was gone as she lay on the table with her breast bared. She stared at the idyllic scene painted on the ceiling, trying not to move, during her daily radiation treatments. She used the time driving to and from treatments to plan her next acquisition. Fatigue would overtake her as she drove home from the hospital, and she welcomed the quiet afternoon to take a short nap. No one ever suspected what she was going through. She was thankful chemotherapy wasn't indicated or required since the biopsy showed the cancer had not spread outside the breast area. Soon, the entire experience was behind her. Except, she would not ignore her health again.

The protocol worked. Soon, Emma was back on schedule—buying, fixing, and renting out properties to new businesses—always careful to protect her identity by telling the sellers she was "helping a friend of the family" with Paul Arnold and Sid Freehling the ones being in the public eye. She went for semiannual exams, kept her appointments, changed her hairstyle to something shorter and easier to maintain, and was feeling younger again.

6

MOVING ON

After three years of being lonely and missing the attentions of a man, she did go on a date with John Davidson, a widower from her Sunday school class.

She and Walter were longtime friends with John and his late wife, so she felt comfortable with him. They went to Greensburg to a movie and stopped at Isaly's for ice cream on the way home. They enjoyed each other's company. After a few months of activities such as church suppers, movies, and companionable evenings just watching TV, John invited her to have Sunday dinner at his house with his three adult children and their spouses.

Although John was pleasant enough to be around, his daughter Mary Jane was determined to be difficult. She resisted sharing her mother's belongings with another woman, objected to Emma sitting where her mother always sat at the table or in the living room, and openly glared at anyone who spoke in a friendly tone to Emma. Mary Jane also made snide remarks about gold-digging widows getting their claws into unsuspecting older men. Emma thought to herself, *Oh, if she only knew!*

Emma and John talked about the evening as he drove her back to her home after dinner. They both saw Mary Jane as a force not to be ignored. They agreed to continue with the friendship aspect and to not get any more involved than an occasional sharing of church events or times when she felt she didn't want to attend a local event unescorted. She didn't like letting Mary Jane win, but Emma was busy enough and a marriage at this point would be a legal complication for her children at her death. Having a prenuptial agreement was something she didn't want to do.

Monday afternoons were when Emma scouted around town looking for properties with signs saying, For sale by owner. She knocked on doors, talking to the owners anxious to sell, saying she was representing Jaroc Enterprises. She arranged for them to see Randall for sales agreements with the actual purchases done by mail or with Randall as power of attorney. All the court documents showed Jaroc Enterprises Inc. as buyer. No one seemed to check who owned Jaroc. Or if they did, they had their money and were leaving town.

Little by little, piece by piece, Emma was improving the town. Houses were being remodeled to have shops on the ground floor. Kitchens were added to second floors or extensions on backs for business owners to have a place to live. New businesses were springing up. The first, a new salon named Hair by Clare, moved into a newly remodeled ground floor with an apartment on the second floor. A ramshackle building was torn down, and a restaurant named The Point was built next to the lake. Ten rental cabins were added, and a campground was in the works.

Another dilapidated building was razed, and Westmoreland County Library opened a branch so new families with children moving into the expanding area had access to a small local inventory and books could be brought in from other branches. Emma finally mustered her courage to go into Walter's library room to sort and donate to the new library most of Walter's collected novels and technical books he read to make up for his lack of education.

Lucerne was being advertised as a weekend getaway for city folks. A few motels were being built after major companies got word of what was happening in Lucerne. Development would take time, but Emma was following her plan. With Randall's help, the plan was working. She was spending more and more time in her little in-town office, establishing an empire to leave to her children who had no idea about any of her activities. For all they knew, she was simply active in her church.

Six months after Emma's corporation bought The Company Store from the mining company, Randall got a call from Mr. Krause, the manager of the store, asking if Randall knew who was buying property in Lucerne. They wanted to sell their house since they were enjoying traveling in their RV and decided to settle in Florida. Of course, Jaroc Enterprises bought the house which the Krause's had rented out rather than leave it sit empty.

Emma had problems with the tenant, a Lisa Weleski, who signed the rental agreement and let her boyfriend, Harold Jeffries, move in later. Emma had her realtor send the traditional certified letter to request evacuation of the property, giving them thirty days and following up with repeated letters when they refused to move out. They kept denying they ever received the repeated letters. After this went on for almost six months, Mr. Arnold had the constable knock on the door to hand them a notice giving them five days to get out. This time, they did, but not before ripping out light fixtures, the kitchen appliances, and the bathroom fixtures. The property was in such disrepair, Emma let the fire department burn it for training purposes, then developed a playground for the children.

Each time Carol visited, she helped clear out more of Walter's belongings, but he lived such a simple life, it didn't take long. Jimbo said he was putting the garage and sheds in order and cleaning his dad's tools.

One weekend, Emma walked out to the shed to see what he was doing. She didn't visit the shed often, considering it Walter's private space he shared with the boys, mostly Jimbo. "Jimbo, since you have done such a great job of cleaning the tools and organizing them, consider them yours."

"Thanks, Ma. I always enjoyed helpin' Dad. I know Robbie didn't like gettin' his hands dirty. Dad and I had some good talks over these tools." Jimbo gave her an unexpected hug, then they both turned to admire his clean workbench.

She continued to rent fields to farmers who harvested hay, grew corn, and planted potatoes. One field became a pasture to some unusual Belted Galloway cattle. Jimbo mowed the lawn, kept cars maintained, and any handyman chores required by living in an old house she kept posted on a list on the front of the refrigerator. Other than his smoking, they shared a peaceful coexistence, with each living their own lives within the same spacious house.

Emma could count on Jimbo to be present at mealtimes if not working at The Company Store. He usually cleared the table after their meals together, placing dishes near the dishwasher. However, they would sit there until she felt like completing the cleanup of the kitchen.

They had their daily routines. She was able to attend to business without him knowing what she was doing all day. She kept the house in order, an easy task with just the two of them and with Jimbo out of the house most of the time. Laundry was done while making phone calls, checking on how Sid was keeping up with building projects.

7

A SCARE

One Friday morning, Emma picked up her Jaroc Enterprise mail at the post office and went up the elevator to her quiet office to make entries in notebooks she kept on each property around town. Just before lunch, she felt faint. She put her head down on her desk until the feeling passed. She had been diligent about keeping all her appointments for follow-up checkups. However, she never felt this way before, and her concern grew. She called Dr. Lawrence and asked when she could be seen again, even though it wasn't time for her regularly scheduled checkup.

At his insistence, she went to see him later that afternoon. There were advantages to living in a small town and being friends with most everyone. Surprisingly, her weight was down. He also noted her pale coloring with a slight yellowing of her skin, indicating a possible jaundice. She felt faint again in his office. Her doctor immediately sent her to the hospital by ambulance to be admitted for tests.

Jimbo was called, and he spent the night slumped in a chair, snoring and keeping her awake, although she doubted she could have slept anyway. She had things to do, people to see. She didn't have time to get sick again. She hoped it could be handled as quickly as her breast cancer episode a few years ago.

"Miz Webster, this is not good news," Dr. Lawrence relayed to her the next morning. "Tests have indicated we are dealing with a far more aggressive kind of cancer this time. It seems there is a tumor on or in your pancreas. We can operate and see how bad it is. I suggest you take a few days and take care of any important matters you have brewing. We will schedule you for surgery on Wednesday if that gives you enough time. Then we will know how to proceed. Until then, take it easy. No driving in case you feel faint again, and check into the hospital Tuesday at three for presurgery tests and preparations. Have a good weekend."

"Easy for you to say, Doc. I'll try to get my projects wrapped up and see you Tuesday." Jimbo drove her home, and he warmed up some leftovers. She didn't feel like eating much, but she forced down some tea and toast and went upstairs to her room, walking slowly through the house, going into the addition to evaluate its condition. She worried about what would happen to this lovely old house without her to fuss over it. She so badly wanted Carol to come back home as Carol, more than the guys, shared her affection for the old house.

She went to church with friends and neighbors Nora and Jake on Sunday, trying to act as though everything were normal. After church, she talked to Randall for advice. He made a suggestion she could initiate. She made sure he was aware of all the properties she was in process of buying.

He tried to assure her. "Now don't worry. I have your power of attorney and will see that your plan goes forward until you can be back at the helm. You know I still have strong feelings for Carol. I won't let anything happen to your investment into her future, or the guys', either. I owe you a debt of gratitude. Just take care of yourself and let me handle everything else." Randall said goodbye with a deep feeling of sadness. After all she had been through, this was not good news. He called Bloomers Flower Shop Monday morning and sent her a bouquet of daisies and carnations, knowing those were her favorites.

On Monday morning, she acted on Randall's suggestion and had Jimbo take her to the courthouse to file for permits to turn the Webster Homestead into a bed-and-breakfast. She feared she wouldn't be around to fulfill that part of her plan, but she hoped it would be what Carol needed to bring her back home to Lucerne where she belonged, not so far away from her roots and people who loved her. Jimbo then dropped her at Randall's office, and she made sure everything was in order in case surgery didn't go well.

"Putting her house in order" was no longer a simple matter. The town was flourishing since she instituted her plan for recovery ten years ago. While there, she went upstairs to her office to write a letter to Randall with an update for her will and listing instructions for him to follow if…she didn't want to think about that eventuality. She put safe deposit box keys, key to the Jaroc office, and the letter to Randall in an envelope and dropped it off with Mamie. Randall was leaving once more, going to Kentucky to help another couple in their pursuit for justice against the coal company there. She asked if Mamie could drive her home, covering the real reason by saying, "My car is in the shop today."

At home, she went through her bedroom and office, leaving notes here and there. She called Carol, telling her about the surgery, who put her life aside and rushed to her mother's side, arriving late evening. Emma made sure the house was as clean as she could leave it, although she didn't feel like cleaning.

8

SADNESS

After Emma's surgery on Wednesday, Dr. Lawrence came out and had a grim talk with Jimbo and Carol, who came up from Virginia thinking it would only be for a few days. "The pancreas was completely involved with cancer, and indications are her liver is also affected. Your mother has only a few weeks, maybe months, at the most. All we can do is keep her comfortable. I'll have full instructions for you on her home care when she is discharged. She made me promise to be honest and direct with her, so I will talk to her when she is awake and able to understand. I gotta hand it to her. She is a strong woman."

While her mother was still in the hospital, Carol drove to Virginia to pack more clothes, prepay some bills, then went back to help out with Ma's care, knowing Jimbo couldn't do this alone. He wasn't the caregiver type. She could continue her writing job from anywhere. At least it was summer, and Susie was out of school and got a job at the new drugstore's counter making ice cream cones and milkshakes. Roberta was away, taking summer college courses.

Carol was concerned with the way Jimbo looked and acted. He was too sullen, too depressed, too drunk most of the time. He barely made an appearance at mealtime, saying he was working late, or left for work in the mornings before Carol could get Ma's breakfast and medications. Carol took her showers when Ma slept after pain meds kicked in or when Betsy, the visiting nurse, stopped by. She and Susie would watch TV in Ma's room until sleep overtook them. Most nights, Carol stayed by her mother's side in case help was needed during the night. As Emma's condition worsened, Jimbo stayed away almost completely, coming home only for a change of clothes, to do his laundry, or sleep.

Emma was very stoic in dealing with her end of life. Nora helped Carol with caring for Emma and some light housework. As Emma grew weaker, spending more and more time in her bedroom, she continued calls to Sid to follow building progress until she was unable to concentrate. She told him, "Let Randall advise you." Carol and her mother got to know each other better than they ever had through long conversations when pain kept Emma from sleeping.

Emma was still trying to convince Carol that she belonged back in Lucerne. "Just try it, honey," Emma would plead. "The girls will be leaving home soon. Who do you have way down there in Virginia, huh? Rob is away from his home so much. Jimbo needs you here. Heaven knows Lucerne needs you." Other times, Emma would go over the interesting history of the house—the generations it sheltered and Pap Webster's loving attention to detail work on trim, stairs, and gingerbread cornices. Church ladies kept a schedule of providing food and relief for the family, endearing themselves to Carol, taking Susie under their wing to provide some entertainment with their own grandchildren. There were a few things, however, Emma still kept silent about, thinking to herself, *She'll find out in due time.*

Before the month was over, Emma Mae Webster was gone, slipping away quietly and full of dignity to the end. Her last words were to tell Carol she loved her and, "Tell your brothers I love them too." And then she barely whispered, "Walter, wait for me. I'll see you soon." Carol was at her side, holding her hand, unable to keep tears at bay.

Carol called Betsy, then Mr. Wolfe, Jimbo at The Store, and Rob before allowing herself to break down and cry in the privacy of her childhood bedroom. When Mr. Wolfe pulled out of the driveway, Carol felt a huge burden fall upon her shoulders. She needed to care for this old house and her little brother Jimbo, who didn't want to be cared for. How was she going to do that from her home in Virginia?

The community turned out full force for Emma's funeral. The line of visitors paying respect during one day of visitation stretched around the block from Wolfe's Funeral Home's door. Carol was so impressed with the small-town support, she was tempted to stay. However, her house and jobs in Virginia were calling her. Rob left a few days after the service to resume his flight schedule.

This was not a good time for her old friend, Randy, Ma's attorney and friend, to be out of town for a trial in Kentucky. She needed answers. She wondered about the ownership of the family home. She knew he was helping her mother with legal matters. Maybe there was a will. Surely Ma would have protected the family homestead she loved so much. Such a grand old house, she didn't want it to fall into unappreciative hands.

Seeing Randy again after all these many years would be extremely difficult. She didn't know how she would feel seeing Randy face to face. She left a message with Mamie for Randy to get in touch with her as soon as he returned to his office. *There is nothing more I can do until I know what, if anything, Ma has arranged for the house's future.*

Carol felt guilty leaving Jimbo, but she just wasn't ready to make drastic changes in her life to return to Lucerne. Carol spent a few days making sure Jimbo had some frozen meals, and she and Susie went back to Virginia. Jimbo would have to start dealing with reality.

PART 2

LATE JUNE–JULY 2015

9

CAROL JEAN WEBSTER MURRAY

When Carol Murray returned from her Saturday afternoon exercise class, where she tried to maintain her trim figure, she greeted the mail carrier descending the steps from her front porch of the small house she rented. "Hello, Henry. How are you today?"

"I'm good, just the same old arthritis kicking up now and again. Important-looking letter for you, Miz Carol," he called over his shoulder as he proceeded toward the next house.

"Thanks, Henry. Not much going on in my life. I hope it brings some good news. Nothing from the IRS, I hope?" Carol didn't mind Henry looking at her mail. A good friend for a long time, she had nothing to hide from him. Her life in Vienna, Virginia, was an open book.

"Nope, some law firm," he said with a grimace as he climbed the neighbors' steps.

Carol opened the front door, and sure enough, there on top of some advertisements spread out on the floor inside the door's mail slot was a letter from a law firm. Not just any law firm. She recognized Randall Block's name immediately. However, she was expecting a call rather than a letter. Randy was a friend from high school days. They once dated; however, she had not seen him since she moved away from Lucerne, Pennsylvania.

Her mother kept her informed of local gossip and told her he did marry, which didn't last. She knew Randy came back to his hometown to hang his shingle after getting his law degree. She hoped the letter contained information about the status of her mother's house, Carol's childhood home. Before she came home after her mother's funeral, she left a message for Randy when he didn't attend the funeral. She opened the envelope and read: "The law office of Randall M. Block, located on 438 Main Street, Lucerne, PA, requests your personal appearance 10:00 am on July 18th, 2015, for the reading of the will of Emma Mae (Smith) Webster. This meeting is very important. Please notify this office of your intent."

Randy personally signed the letter with a handwritten PS: "My condolences on the loss of your mother. Sorry I missed seeing you while you were here in town. I am looking forward to seeing you again. I'll answer in person any questions you might have." Just seeing his personal scrawl at the bottom of the official letter was enough to bring back memories, both good and bad. There was a time when their friendship was blossoming into a romance, leading them toward the altar in Fellowship Presbyterian Church where they were both members.

She eased into a nearby chair, holding his letter, while her thoughts went back to the past. She remembered how much of a gentleman Randy was with good manners, a deep faith in God, devotion to his parents, helpfulness to his sisters, and was a great athlete. He was competitive and good-looking in football, basketball, or softball uniforms. The cheerleaders all harbored crushes on him.

He was focused on going to college and competed with her brother, Rob, for an athletic scholarship. When Randy won, Rob joined the Air Force. Rob made her life miserable while he was still home by tormenting her about being a traitor for the short time she still dated Randy. Seeing her relationship with Randy was too complicated, she broke it off, something she ended up regretting.

About the same time as the breakup with Randy, Theodore Murray came into her life with his promise of taking her away from the coal town where she grew up. He was a traveling salesman for Lambert's Mercantile Company, supplying The BNP Company Store with fabrics and notions. When ladies needed yard goods for making dresses for themselves or children, or material for quilts, Ted took their requests and brought their orders two weeks later. The ladies were always asking, "When is Teddy coming back?"

She never understood why Ted took a liking to her. The truth of the matter, she didn't realize how attractive she was. Carol, at five feet four inches tall, was quite a striking young lady with her natural blond hair, big blue eyes, and trim figure which was a result of working hard on their small farm on the edge of town where she lived with her parents and two brothers, Robert (Robbie) and James (Jimbo). Her father worked in the coal mine, and a lot of the farming was left to Ma and young folks. They grew vegetables Ma canned to see them through winter. Cows and chickens provided milk, butter, and eggs. Sheep and goats were tended and required lots of work. She helped her mother clean the great, old house and care for her grandparents.

Carol fell victim to Ted's smooth-talking ways and was soon in "a delicate condition." She quit her job as a waitress in a diner out on the four-lane highway and left town with Ted after a quick courthouse ceremony with only family in attendance. She was embarrassed about how quickly she left, not saying goodbye to anyone. She knew marrying a man she barely knew was quite a gamble.

Ted moved her into his efficiency apartment in Vienna, Virginia, a small town in the Washington, DC, suburbs. She redecorated his bachelor pad to be as homey as possible on her limited means. Ted was rarely home since his job required him to continue traveling, leaving her alone. She felt abandoned. She also suspected he used his smooth-talking ways on other women on his sales route.

A nearby town had a beauty school where Carol went to get an inexpensive haircut instead of always doing her long, blond hair into a ponytail each day. She started taking more pride in her personal appearance. When at home, she still dressed in her favorite garb of jeans and a comfortable T-shirt. However, when she did go out, she wore polyester slacks and a knit shirt from JCPenney, which was all she could afford. She attended business classes and a writing class at the local community college during her pregnancy. Getting out of Lucerne showed her another way of life away from coal mining without the sadness of watching the area being destroyed and without having to watch her daddy dying a slow death. She missed her family, but she was determined to make her marriage work in spite of it all.

She waited two months after the first baby was born, named Roberta in honor of an uncle and her brother Robert, to send birth announcements so no one would know about her sin before marriage. The baby girl was small. No one back home would know her true birth date. Rob was away in the Air Force. Later, Jimbo joined the Navy soon after he graduated from high school and the mines closed, ending his job delivering coal. She wasn't the only one who wanted to get out of Lucerne.

Shortly after their second baby was born, two uniformed police officers knocked on her door. "Ma'am, are you Mrs. Theodore Murray?"

"Yes, I am, officer. If you are looking for him, he isn't home."

"We aren't looking for him, ma'am. We are sorry to inform you, your husband was climbing on a lattice porch enclosure when the homeowner fired a warning shot at what he thought was an intruder. If the bullet didn't kill him, the fall onto the concrete did. I'm so sorry, ma'am. You need to go to Holidaysburg up in Pennsylvania to identify and claim the body. We will arrange transportation for you if you want."

Carol, with tears streaming, replied, "Thanks anyway. I'll drive there and make arrangements. He has no other family." The officers made sure she was calm and in control before they left her, giving her a number to call if she needed help.

When Ted was laid to rest, using all their meager savings, Carol reevaluated her life: two children to feed and raise alone and a small rental house they moved into when they found out they were having a second baby. There was a life insurance policy, at least. Her part-time job at the library allowed her to take Baby Susie to work while Roberta went to playtime at the church nursery school. She also wrote freelance articles for *The Star*, a local newspaper, and had several short stories published in magazines. She would be able to survive while raising her children. She was determined to never fall for idle promises again.

She wondered whether she should go back to Lucerne to at least be closer to family, then decided against it. She didn't want to admit her errors in a small town where everyone's business was known. She managed to survive and went back for short visits, for her father's funeral, and ten years later, to attend to her mother which ended with another funeral. Lucerne represented sadness to her.

She struggled to bring her thoughts back to the present day. All evening, Carol wondered what was so important about her mother's will she had to attend in person. She took care of her mother during her final days and attended her mother's funeral two weeks ago. Her mother didn't indicate there was anything important for her to know.

After rereading Randy's letter about reading Ma's will, Carol dashed off a quick email to Randy's law firm. "I will be attending the reading of my mother's will. I doubt the will is so important, except for property and house. But I will certainly be there." Thinking to herself, *There was the Ford Fusion Ma must have bought with Dad's insurance money. I might ask for that to be part of my inheritance.* She turned off the computer, leaned back in her chair, and let her mind wander back again to Lucerne days.

Randy was an important part of her old life, and she wondered what it would be like seeing him again. Her mother kept telling her, "Randall is successful, Carol. He is so helpful when I have any legal matters. He stops in to keep me company sometimes. It's lonely here all by myself." Ma was always asking her to come home. Now, Ma was gone. Although she wanted to go back, she wondered how she could face her former friends. Too many questions would be asked. She was too embarrassed to admit her condition when she married Ted to get out of Lucerne. He was just a ticket for escape.

Things are different now. What would it be like to go back? What is there to go back to? My children have their own lives, and the rental is month to month on my small house. "I'll think about that later," she said aloud, although no one was there to hear her.

She went for a brisk walk, and then called her brother Rob who flew for United Airlines.

10

ROBERT CLAIR WEBSTER

Rob opened the door to his luxury condo unit in Reston, Virginia, rolled in his luggage wheelies, and picked up mail from the foyer table where his latest "roomie" placed it. Just then, his cell phone rang. He nearly fell over some suitcases left near the door, switched the mail to his other hand, and saw the caller identification said Carol Murray. He juggled everything in his hands to answer his cell phone. "Hi, sis. What's up?"

"Have you received a letter from Randy Block about needing to go to Lucerne for the reading of Ma's will? Did you even know she had a will?"

"Hold on, Carol. I just got in the door from my flight. Yes, there is a letter here from Randall Block's law firm. What does it say exactly? I can't juggle my telephone and read the mail."

She read her letter to him. "The law office of Randall M. Block, located on 438 Main Street, Lucerne, PA, requests your personal appearance 10:00 am on July 18th, 2015, for the reading of the will of Emma Mae (Smith) Webster. This meeting is very important. Please notify this office of your intent."

Rob grumbled, "Just what I don't need—another trip back to Lucerne so soon! It's only been two weeks since the funeral. Why wasn't this done then?"

Carol continued, "Randy was out of town, remember? He didn't pay respects. I can arrange time off from my jobs if I work long hours between now and then, but my old Camry might give me problems. I don't think it will make another trip up there and back. An airline ticket and rental car would be hard on my finances right now. Roberta's schooling is costing me a bundle, and Susie wants to go to college too. Is there any chance of a companion pass on your airline?"

"Let me get back to you on the pass. I am starting my month-long vacation on July 1. I did hope to do anything other than go to Lucerne, but that won't take much time. I am exhausted now. I need some sleep. May I call you tomorrow about 1000 hours? Give me time to see what is going on here with these suitcases in the foyer, make some calls, and develop a plan."

Later, after a brief conversation with his "roomie," a shower to wash away the grit from a rough flight schedule, sleep evaded him as he recalled all the many reasons he hated going to Lucerne. He got back up out of bed to sit in his cozy kitchen, read the mail, drink coffee, and relive the past.

The coal mine dominated the hometown as he was growing up. His father, Walter, worked for the coal company for forty years, driving the motor to haul miners into the mines in the morning. His father told them of miners opening dinner buckets on the way into the mine and eating desserts first in case they didn't live long enough to eat dessert after they ate their sandwiches. Coal dust surrounded them, got inside their mouths, and spoiled the taste of food. After miners got to work, the motor hauled loads of mined coal and rock that was dumped onto conveyors to be sorted by young boys. The last load of the day would be to bring miners out at shift change after a hard day of using picks to open veins and shovels to load their required amount. Some men drilled holes and tamped in explosives to loosen coal veins.

His dad came home filthy too, although he didn't actually dig for coal. Only skin around his eyes was still recognizable where goggles protected from thick black dust. He would go down to the basement sink to wash where Ma kept a change of clothes for him so he wouldn't bring coal dust into the house. As it turned out, coal dust settled into his dad's lungs, causing so much damage that he died an early, excruciatingly painful death. Basically, he suffocated, unable to draw oxygen into his damaged lungs. A bout with TB and a simple cold complicated his condition. However, black lung caused his death.

His dad expected Rob would follow in the footsteps of a long family line of miners. However, Rob never had any intentions of becoming a miner. He worked hard in school athletics to earn a college scholarship. When Randy Block got the scholarship, Rob went to the recruiting office in Greensburg and volunteered for the Air Force. After the first year, he applied for officer school and pilot training so he could get as far away as possible from mining.

He wouldn't even think of going back to Lucerne to live. He barely tolerated required visits. He liked his luxurious life just fine. He raised his hands to admire his clean fingernails, something his father never could do. Rob's good job with a major airline and living in a condo meant no home maintenance to worry about. Every other week when at home, he had a manicure by Janet, a talented young lady. If he was out of town when his nails needed to be done, he went to Pamela in Denver, Maria in Dallas, and Justin in San Francisco. Once a month, he included a pedicure. He had his favorite hairstylist in different cities too.

Women practically fawned over him, at five foot eleven inches tall, since he inherited his mother's Smith genes: full-headed blond hair; good-looking, dreamy blue eyes; and athletic build. He had his own private airplane for tooling around on more-than-adequate time off. What more could a guy want? His sister, Carol, lived close enough to see her when he desired family time yet far enough away she didn't interfere in his life.

When the coffeepot was empty, he went back to bed. After a short night of some fitful sleep and some quick phone calls in the morning, Rob called Carol as promised at 1000 hours. (He still used Greenwich time as it was used in his job with the airlines.) She answered after two rings. "Good morning, Carol. Sorry I was so abrupt yesterday. I was beat after flying through that East Coast cold front yesterday. I had four legs up and down through it, with delays, and…well, you probably don't want to hear about it. I tried telling Angela last night, and she just rolled her eyes and said, 'Is that all you can talk about—airplanes or flying or where you are going next or the cute flight attendants you fly with?' She was already packed and left without so much as a kiss goodbye. She handed me the condo key, saluted, called me Captain Wonderful in a sarcastic tone, and left, slamming the door behind her. Good riddance!

"Which means, dear sister, I am free once more. You know I don't want to go to Lucerne to see that blasted Randy Block. You know I have a problem with that guy. He got the athletic scholarship I wanted. Because of him, I couldn't go to college. I knew our folks didn't have enough money. The military was my only choice."

Carol got a chance to speak while Rob fumed. "Then shouldn't you thank him? If you didn't join the Air Force, would you have learned to fly and would you be doing what you do now? You would be a beat-up athlete."

Rob admitted, "I guess you have a point. I'll back off. He's only doing his job. Getting back to the trip to Lucerne, why don't you drive out to Dulles and we can go to Lucerne together in my *Bonanza* the morning of the sixteenth, weather permitting? I will fly us up and back. We can land at the new airport on the north side of town where Westmoreland County built an airport on one of those flattened mountaintops created by strip mining. That will give us a chance to talk to Jimbo ahead of the reading to see what he knows, if anything."

"Oh Rob, that would solve several problems. That would be great."

"I will get a companion pass for you in the system with United in case weather isn't suitable. Go straight to the gate and give them your name and my seniority number, 722520. We'll stay in touch between now and then. Have a good day."

He barely gave her time to say, "Thanks, Rob. I owe you one. Bye." He made another call to arrange her companion pass and flipped through his black book for someone to accompany him on his vacation to France.

11

RANDALL MAXWELL BLOCK

Randy, as most locals and friends called him since school days, sat at his office desk on Wednesday, June 24, 2015, getting papers in order for several pending trials. He dressed every day in a business suit, white shirt, and tie, although his tie was loosened and his suit coat hung over the back of his chair.

He could straighten his tie and put on his jacket at a moment's notice to present an authoritative, professional image. Miz Emma Mae Smith Webster's last will and testament was uppermost in his mind, making other business less important for the time being. He was still distracted by Carol's email, knowing she would be returning to town in three weeks. Randy wasn't over his friendship with Carol, although he tried with a law-school classmate. His ex-wife was too career oriented and hated living in Lucerne for the short time she did. So far, no other woman measured up to his standards.

His work kept him busy. On weekends, he maintained the old family home he inherited after his folks died. His father was a thirty-five-year coal miner, dead from black lung disease, and his mother was killed in a car accident trying to get away from what she called "this godforsaken town."

Ruth Maxwell Block never got used to living in a coal mining town in spite of her love for Randy's father, Joseph. They met during his two-year Army stint at Fort Dix, New Jersey. She was a student at Princeton University and headed for a summer concert tour as an accomplished pianist immediately after graduation. When she was hired to entertain soldiers on base at Christmas, she met Joseph and they fell in love.

She married Joseph as soon as her concert tour was completed, giving up a promising career by moving to Lucerne. She contented herself by playing piano at church and giving piano lessons to her own children and any other child whose family could afford a few dollars a week. She raised their three children, was a devoted wife and mother, and tolerated deplorable conditions in Lucerne for her husband's sake as long as he was alive. She said goodbye to Randy and left as soon as she was free to go. She was moving to Florida to be closer to a daughter when a drunk driver couldn't handle mountain roads and smashed both of them to kingdom come.

Randy's mind kept wandering through the past, disrupting his focus on legal briefs. After his mother died so tragically, he decided to look after Carol's mother who was left alone after her husband died a horrible death, as did his father, barely able to breathe due to lung damage from working in the mines. Miz Emma was a fine Christian lady. He was proud to represent the Websters, while Walter was still alive, in a lawsuit against the BNP Coal Company. He helped them make out their wills to protect those winnings. That way, he could keep up with Carol and what was going on in her life. He felt closer to Carol through Miz Emma talking about her.

Miz Emma's children had been all out of town for a time. Rob went into the Air Force then became an airline pilot living in another state. Carol left suddenly after a courthouse marriage ceremony with a traveling salesman and was probably too embarrassed to come back after a scandal about her husband being shot and killed. Jimbo, the youngest child, joined the Navy. When Jimbo was discharged from military service, he moved in with his mother and did little except cause trouble. Randy backed off his frequent visits, but not on his caring for her. Jimbo wasn't as caring a son as Randy felt he could have been, so Randy still took care of her important business and tried to be a substitute big brother to Jimbo.

Randy buzzed for his secretary. When Mamie came in, he looked up from his paperwork and asked, "Won't the Webster siblings be surprised when I read Miz Emma's will? Could you please set up dinner reservations for five at six thirty on July 18 at The Point? I'd like you to go along since you know as much about Miz Emma's legal matters as I do, and I may need your assistance dealing with all three of them at once."

Mamie stood in front of his desk, noticing his tired eyes. "Certainly, Randy. I mean, Mr. Block. Sorry. I would be pleased to be included. Is there anything else you need before I leave?"

"That's okay, Mamie. You may call me Randy. That is all for today, except for dropping off mail at the post office. I need to deliver this one in person," he groaned as he picked up one envelope and put it into his jacket pocket. He watched as she gathered together a stack of mail and turned to go back to her desk where she shouldered her purse before walking out the door with a little wave goodbye.

He couldn't ask for a better secretary. She was more than that, he realized. With her Irish red hair and green eyes, she was as much a friend as she was a secretary. She attended law school at night, and he looked forward to hiring her as his associate. He figured Miss Mamie McMillen would be a great lawyer someday. He just hoped she didn't find that Prince Charming she mentioned a few times for which she was looking. *What would I do if I lost her? Finding a replacement would be impossible. Back to work*, he reminded himself as he bent his head over the stack of files on his desk.

He kept an eye on the clock as he wanted to hand deliver Jimbo Webster's letter about reading Miz Emma's will before Jimbo closed The Company Store for the day. Lately, Jimbo wasn't quite the same, losing interest in life itself. There were a few speeding tickets, and as prearranged, the bartender called Randy to give Jimbo a ride home from the tavern one night when it was obvious Jimbo shouldn't be driving.

Whether Jimbo liked it or not, Randy was looking out for him by keeping an eye on him and his increasingly dark moods. He was worried Jimbo might do something drastic since his lack of caring about himself was getting too obvious. Although having a beer now and then didn't hurt anyone, Jimbo had been seen hanging around the tavern a little too often and too late at night since Miz

Webster's funeral. His casual drinking was turning into something to be watched. Knowing what he did about how a college roommate behaved before he "fell" off a bridge, he didn't want anything to happen to Jimbo at this critical time. He would talk to Rob and Carol when they were back for reading of the will to see what they thought.

With the day's work done, cases filed, and Mamie taking outgoing mail to the post office, he closed his office, knowing the evening would be a difficult one. As he walked toward The Company Store, he realized how much the town was really changing. He was happy about being a small part of what was happening.

The town was no longer smoky with everything coated with soot since coke ovens shut down when the mines closed. He remembered when his grandparents painted their house white and it turned gray with soot and dust in a few days. The trees in autumn colors would be vibrant again. He hated the mines, too, knowing personally how devastating the effects of mining could be. He wished his mother could see the town now. He took a deep breath of clean, fresh air.

His grandfather and father had been miners. Randy worked in the mines the summer of his fourteenth birthday to help out financially. Back in 1885, the law stated boys as young as twelve could work in the mines. In 1902, the age was raised to fourteen. However, fathers in need of additional financial support could go to the mine office and get a blank certificate and make his son any age he wanted him to be.

There were children as young as five and six working different jobs in and around the mines. In some mines where there wasn't a motor, there were also nippers, young boys whose job it was to open and close heavy doors that let cars full of coal pass through mine tunnels. These doors were normally kept closed to control ventilation within the mine. Nippers had to be quick and alert. A coal car weighing around four tons crashing through an unopened door could be disastrous.

There were also spraggers—agile and quick boys who put logs, called sprags, into moving wheels of coal cars not towed by a motor to slow them down as they rolled by gravity through the mines. They had to be accurate or run the risk of losing fingers. As they grew older, some boys were trained to drive mules in some parts of the mine to haul coal cars unable to use gravity. These mules lived in the mines, never seeing light of day.

The boys learned early to chew tobacco, which was said to keep coal dust from going down their throats. Of course, this wasn't effective and only created another habit with inherent dangers.

Randy's job as a breaker boy was to sort out slate and other non-coal material as coal rolled down a chute. Sitting on planks astride coal chutes, bent over nearly in half, breaker boys used their feet to "break" the flow of coal to perform their jobs. None of the boys were allowed to wear gloves since it slowed down their sorting process. Their fingertips were cracked and bled until built-up calluses hardened them.

Although their work was back breaking, coal dust and boyish pranks were nearly as bad. They were a rowdy bunch. Although his athletic build was strong enough, working all day in the coal business took a mind-set Randy did not have. He required sunshine and clean air to breathe. He was relieved when his parents insisted they could manage without his contribution after a close call when a collapsing coal chute killed a boy next to him. His short experience was enough to inspire him to work harder when he went back to school that fall.

Randy went into his freshman year and buckled down to make something of himself to get out of the mining mentality of *It's my destiny. There isn't anything else I qualify for. If it was good enough for Dad, it's good enough for me!* No, sir.

He played as many sports as he could in high school, focusing on earning a scholarship since he knew his folks couldn't afford any further education for him. What he lacked in stature, he made up in speed and endurance. He won the scholarship, applied to Indiana University of Pennsylvania, and worked evenings and weekends making leather wallets in a factory to make ends meet.

After college, he worked part time as a law clerk and attended classes at Pennsylvania School of Law in Philadelphia. After graduation, he came home to Lucerne to hang his shingle on a vacant storefront office to help miners in their quest for judgments against coal companies for wrongful death. He set up satellite offices in several Pennsylvania cities, partnering with several former law school classmates.

He earned his private pilot license and used his four-seat, single-engine Piper Cherokee 140 to travel between offices if weather permitted. He was also a consultant in an office in Wheeling, West Virginia, and another in Roanoke, Virginia. He only visited there occasionally to check on proceedings. The internet was a huge help lately. Although the coal industry was decreasing, down 37 percent, there were still fifty thousand miners in the country fighting for their rights.

The local folks in Lucerne were his personal clients. He took care of legal matters for everyone. A small town like Lucerne, Pennsylvania, did not attract lawyers in search of big dollars. He, assisted by Mamie and an intern, handled a heavy workload since they were the only law firm in town. He had so much work. He did exceedingly well, indeed, while staying true to the simple life that brought him home to Lucerne and kept him here after his father died of the dreaded black lung disease and his mother's accident.

His walk to The Company Store was completed. He handed the letter about reading Miz Emma's will to Jimbo, which almost turned his stomach seeing Jimbo looking so sullen and depressed, thinner than usual, with his hair way too long and greasy, hanging over his eyes. All Randy could see was an unshaven chin above a dirty shirt with shirttail untucked from dirty jeans with one torn knee.

12

JAMES ALAN WEBSTER

Carol and Rob's younger brother, James, more commonly called Jimbo, worked at The Company Store in Lucerne, which was managed by Artie and Evelyn Krause. The Krauses decided to retire, buy an RV, and travel after Jaroc Enterprises Inc. bought the property when the mining company moved out of town. Jimbo received a letter from Jaroc asking him to stay on to run the store. He sent his rent check to a post office box. It was a job! Kept him in beer and cigarettes, and the VA took care of his medical needs.

Jimbo, slouched on a stool behind the register, received his hand delivered letter about the reading of Ma's will as Randy stopped by for some nails and glue for a bookcase he was building. He glanced at the envelope Randy handed him and asked, "What's this all about?" as he reached out with one hand to take the envelope from Randy while scratching his two weeks' growth of whiskers with the other.

Randy quipped, "Read it. I think you can understand plain English."

"I don't think your kind knows how to use plain English." Jimbo, squinting through bloodshot eyes, frowned instantly as he read, "The law office of Randall Block, located on 438 Main Street, Lucerne, PA, requests your personal appearance, 10:00 am on July 18th, 2015, for the reading of the will of Emma Mae (Smith) Webster. This meeting is very important. Please notify this office of your intent."

Jimbo was not thrilled by the long-reaching impact of this letter. "You mean my brother and sister will be comin' again? I avoided a scene when they were here for Ma's funeral. I may not be so nice next time. I don't need them nosin' around my business." His dark-brown eyes seemed to get darker as he peered out from under a mane of black hair hanging over his bushy eyebrows. "Ma didn't have anythin' to make a fuss over. Why are you doin' this?"

"Like it or not, Rob and Carol have responded they will be arriving on July 16, possibly the seventeenth. You'd better make nice, get their old rooms ready, and for heaven's sake, clean up your act for a few days. If I hadn't been out of town most of June including the week of Miz Emma's funeral, I would have taken care of reading her will at that time. As it is, this is a necessary meeting. Trust me, you need to get dried out, detoxed, or whatever the hell you have to do. Shape up or ship out, mate. Shave off that grungy beard, take a bath, and for God's sake, get that mop cut that is on top of your head. Look respectable for a change. I am concerned about you. I promised Miz Emma to look after you. I aim to keep my word. How many times have I told you to take better care of yourself?"

Jimbo crumpled the letter and tossed it into his trash can. "I'll be there, buddy. Never fear. Jimbo can handle those two all the longer they will be in town. They will run faster than a jackrabbit after the readin' is finished. They are both such pantywaists, they can't handle life in Lucerne. Hell, who can? You are getting like an old nag. I am taking care of myself. Get off my back, Randy. You don't care if I am alive or dead, *mate!*"

"You have three weeks, Jimbo. Only three weeks. I'll nag you until you do something so you are around to see what the future has in store. Get a grip, please. You need to break some bad habits before they get too serious."

Randy wandered through the old store, noting old, dusty stock. Whatever anyone needed, The Company Store had it. Most locals came in for their basic needs instead of going to big-box stores up the road in Indiana, Pennsylvania. Everyone in town knew everyone else and everyone's business too. Jimbo might be a bit cantankerous, but he was really a good soul like most local folks, if he didn't let his drinking for companionship get the best of him. Randy made his purchase and left the store, coughing to clear his throat of inhaled dust.

Jimbo watched Randy leave and then picked Randy's letter back out of the trash can, smoothed out the wrinkles against his pant leg, then folded it and angrily shoved it in his shirt pocket. When he closed up, Jimbo took his letter home and posted it on the front of the refrigerator, reading and rereading it over the next few days, getting more agitated as time progressed.

On Saturday, he closed the store a little early when customers dwindled and only a few old geezers were telling stories on the bench outside. Jimbo locked the door, dropped the day's receipts into the new branch bank's night deposit, and then moseyed down to the tavern. He would rather drink his supper than face that old house he still lived in since no one told him to move out. Living there was free, and he did not see any other option. Rents on new apartments were reasonable, but it didn't match free.

He lived with his mother, until she died, in a house too big for the two of them, mowed lawn, and fixed things needing to be fixed on a list she kept posted on the refrigerator. "What's the big deal?" he used to ask. "It's just an old house. No need to be so particular." Now that she was gone, walls echoed with her sayings, her pious attitude, her incriminating looks. Maybe Ma's last will and testament would answer his question about whether he could continue to stay in the family home or have to move, sell, whatever.

From his favorite perch at Mike's Tavern, he mumbled into his beer. "Can't a guy live how he wants to?" To the regular guy occupying a stool at the end of the bar, he complained, "I tried minin'. I tried to follow destiny down that black hole in the ground. I couldn't stand it. I quit that nonsense after two long days. I didn't care about money miners made. Dad was lucky to drive the motor in and out all day long. At least he occasionally got a breath of decent air. I tried drivin' truck to deliver coal to residents of towns up and down the valley. That's when I was constantly propositioned by all those lonely women whose husbands were killed while minin', or too sick or too tired to do what men are supposed to do for their wives.

"I served my four years in the Navy. All I got for that was a medal for bravery and a leg injury from trippin' over an anchor chain after a night of shore leave drinkin' with the guys. I couldn't get home for Dad's funeral since we were out playin' war games. Hell, comin' back to Lucerne was my only option. I was glad the mines were closed down. I would have refused to go back into those damned mines. Runnin' The Company Store suits me. Minimum wage buys my beer and a few groceries. What more do I need? Everyone thinks I am a drug addict. I just take those pills the VA gives me for my leg pain."

The bartender came by to refresh their drafts and discuss the booming business since the old, worked-out mine was opened as a tourist attraction. People who had no idea what miners did back then were taking joyrides in and out of the shallow entrance to the mine where it had been shored up to prevent any cave-ins such as miners feared. No tourist went deep enough to get full effect of what miners really experienced.

The local mines, besides being worked out, were shut down after the Occupational Safety and Health Administration (OSHA) declared the hazards of mining weren't worth the risk to human life. New laws governing mining operations combined with local residents and steel mills converting to natural gas made mining less than profitable. Sharp lawyers like Randy were winning too many lawsuits on behalf of black lung sufferers.

"Hell, my old man died from black lung disease. Had tuberculosis, too; spent some time at Cresson Sanatorium while he was so contagious. That's when I was leavin' for the Navy, you know. Left Ma all alone in that ole house. My old man escaped from Cresson one cold night just before Thanksgiving. Came home in pajamas after hitchhikin' all that way. His lungs were so damaged, a simple cold put him in the ground. Don't talk to me about how good those worked-out mines are for local economy. This town is dead. May as well blow it to smithereens. Sometimes, I feel as dead as this ole town." The bartender walked away, leaving Jimbo alone to drown his misery in his mug of beer.

Jimbo sat there nursing his beers, one after another, until he knew he had to go home and start getting the house gussied up for

His and Her Majesty coming back to visit in less than three weeks. When he got home, he did take off his work shoes and put on slippers he kept at the door like Ma made him do to protect hardwood floors. He looked around the family home, made a list of things needing attention again so soon after their last visit, and microwaved some leftover funeral casserole he found stashed in the freezer. He downed two more beers before settling his six-foot, lanky frame in front of the TV where he fell asleep in Ma's recliner, still dressed in his Levi's and Wool Rich shirt. He didn't have enough gumption to go upstairs to take a shower or sleep in his bedroom.

Waking at four in the morning, he worked a cramp out of his neck from recliner sleeping and started upstairs. He lit a cigarette and formed a different thought in his booze-numbed mind. He sat down on a stair tread to contemplate. He asked the echoing voices, "Why do I need to keep this old, drafty house in good shape? Ma is gone. His and Her Majesty can stay at Motel 6 on the north side of town. Randy can't order me around. I don't have any good reason to change my life. What if…"

He went into the kitchen and rummaged in the trash bin for some papers to dump onto the couch. Next, he went to the garage to get a can of gasoline but then mumbled to himself, "Nope, bad idea. The fire chief will easily figure out gasoline was used as an accelerant." So he went back inside. "I'll just make it look as though I fell asleep with a lit cigarette. No one will miss the house or me. I'll make sure any neighbors, especially Nora and Jake Simpson across the road, aren't home in case the fire spreads. No use takin' anyone else along on my final journey."

He stomped his way upstairs and sprawled on his bed with his clothes on to sleep for a few hours. Since it was Sunday morning, no one expected him to open the store until one. By then, it would be all over. He was sorry sirens of fire trucks would disturb church services. He could picture all the volunteers in dress clothes, running outdoors. "Preachers and priest may as well quit preachin' after volunteers empty pews."

*****

Jimbo heard the neighbors across the road leave for church at nine thirty. That was his cue to carry some valuables out to the back garage and put them into his aged Bronco. He parked Ma's car next to the back garage. He mumbled to himself as he walked back and forth, *Carol will want Ma's handmade quilts, the photo albums, and Ma's silver tea set she kept polished for when church ladies came over. Robbie will want trophies from his room he earned from all the athletic accomplishments and Dad's gold watch awarded when he retired from minin'.*

He remembered how Robbie and Randy were on the same football, basketball, and softball teams all through school. *Didn't like each other then, and the feeling is still mutual. That's why I never tried out for any sports teams. I knew I couldn't compare to my big brother.* It was enough when one teacher actually said to him, "You'll never be the man your brother is."

He made a pot of coffee, poured one last mug full, carried it into the living room, sat down on the couch, and pulled a cigarette from a half-empty pack. He tapped it on the coffee table and picked up a book of matches from a crystal bowl on the coffee table that he recalled being filled with candies on his Grammie Smith's coffee table.

Reading the name on the matchbook, he recalled picking up those matches at Peg and Elmo's restaurant. Dad, Robbie, and he used to stop on the way home from the lake for a barbecued ham sandwich back when Robbie was still home. The three guys would take the Jon boat and fish all day on Sundays. Those were great times. *Too many memories of the past. Get on with it*, he chided himself for getting sentimental.

He lit a match and dropped it on trash papers piled on the couch. While he waited for flames to catch, he laid his head on the couch's high back, remembering how they would light a campfire and cook the morning's catch in Crisco and an old skillet Dad carried in his old Jeep. They would throw some potatoes into the fire and, in corn season, wet some ears of corn still in the husk and throw those in too. Dad would say, "Don't need no womenfolk to feed us when a man knows how to fish." The boys would agree and dig in.

*****

"What the hell?" he yelled when he awoke, still holding an unlit cigarette and that book of matches. He actually did fall asleep as he planned, but the match went out when a tiny flame reached paper with soggy coffee grounds stuck on the underside. There was no fire, just scorched paper. He brought the book of matches up in front of his eyes to read the name again, and the name blurred through misty eyes. *I must have some guardian angel watchin' over me.*

He struck another match to light his cigarette, declaring it would be his last one, but not because he wasn't going to be around. He was determined to do what Randy was constantly nagging him about: "Clean up your act." Jimbo realized he wanted to have a son, maybe a daughter, someday so he could pass along to his child what he learned from his dad. He waited until the cigarette was nearly burning his fingers before he stubbed it out. The coffee in his mug was cold, and the old house was still intact. "God help me," he said as he stood, stretched, and muttered to himself as he went out to his Bronco and brought items he stashed there back into the house and put them where they belonged. With another look around the rooms, he declared, "I can do this."

The trash from the couch went back to the kitchen trash can, and he tried to ignore what he hoped would be his final morning-after headache as he read over his list of things to do around the house before his siblings' visit. He had a lot to do. He numbered the priorities and stuck the list on the refrigerator next to Randy's letter. He would cross off items as they were completed.

Jimbo went upstairs to shower and shave. He gave himself a good looking over in the full-length mirror in Ma's room. He didn't like what he saw. "Look at yourself, Jimbo," he said to his image. "Your hair is too long, your eyes are sunken with dark circles, you have lost too much weight by living on your liquid meals. Shape up, sailor." He added, "Lord help me get through this," as he dressed for work. He chose clean jeans, a bright yellow shirt, and promised himself to do what Randy said—shape up.

He barely got through the workday. As he closed up, he gathered the day's receipts and felt totally washed out. He locked the doors, dropped the money bag in the night deposit slot at the bank, and took the familiar walk in the door at Mike's Tavern. He sat down in his regular stool and greeted the regulars with a nod. When the bartender came for his order, Jimbo said, "I'll have a…a…black coffee, and make that to go. Sorry, Charlie, you are losing a good customer." He tossed a couple of bills on the bar, picked up his coffee, waved goodbye with a "See ya," and hurried out the door before he lost his nerve. Hard work is what he needed to keep his mind and hands busy.

He pulled out his cell phone and called Randy. "Randy, my friend. I need help. I promised myself I could do what you said, but I can't do it alone. Could you meet me back at the house in a little while unless you have something more pressin' to do?"

Randy was pleased to be asked for help. "Sure. I was wondering what I was going to do this evening. See you in a bit."

Jimbo went back to The Company Store and took stock of his paint supply. He chose some soft colors and the supplies needed to start giving the house a brighter look. He loaded everything in his old Bronco. He tallied up the cost of everything and left an IOU in the empty cash drawer, scribbling a note to himself so he could write out a check in the morning. By the time he got home, Randy was sitting on the porch swing, but he wasn't alone. "We don't need no one else, mate."

"You remember Mamie, don't ya? I told her where I was going when I saw her on my way over. She offered to help. Never hurts to have a female's perspective. She already has her steno pad out making notes about things to do outside. Come on, mate. Let her help."

"Okay. Just don't get in the way." Jimbo opened the door then stepped aside for them to enter. He drained his container of coffee and went to make more.

Mamie continued making notes as Jimbo began to give them a rundown on what he planned to do. He excused himself to go change into a pair of cut-off jeans and found large handkerchiefs for everyone to cover their hair. Mamie kept quiet and out of the way but was forming some ideas of her own. She folded outdated bedding, took down old posters and dusty curtains, and helped move all the furniture into the center of the room before covering everything with drop cloths. She picked up a screwdriver and removed electrical outlet and switch covers in the targeted rooms. When the guys started to paint, she wandered through the house, taking notes on ways to brighten and improve the decor. She found some Old English Scratch Cover in the closet off the kitchen and went to work.

Randy came downstairs at ten. "I'm going to hit the hay, Mamie. Let me give you a lift home?"

Mamie put everything away and gratefully accepted the ride. "Sure. I'm tired too. Also, I still have a paper to do for law class. Let me wash my hands and say goodbye to Jimbo."

Jimbo thanked them for their help, not noticing what Mamie had done to the furniture in the living room and dining room. He was so wired from the coffee he drank all evening and the sugar overload from the hard candies to numb his desire to smoke that he went back upstairs and did a second coat on the ceilings. At midnight, he dropped into bed, exhausted, but pleased with what he already accomplished, thanks to all the help.

He got up in the morning and noticed his hands shaking. *Is that from too much caffeine?* he wondered. But he didn't know how else to deal with his cravings. He put in another day at work, accepting Randy's offer to help again this evening.

Mamie dropped in later just as they were finishing the walls in the first room. She had two bags in one hand and a sketch pad tucked under her arm. "I know you told me to stay out of your way. I don't want to impose, but I have some sketches and samples I want to show you of what this house could and should look like. Here, eat some hamburgers and fries while I show you." She amazed the guys with her ideas as she flipped through the sketches. She was not only easy on the eyes with her Irish red hair and green eyes but she was also a talented designer.

"When did you have time to do all this?" Randy asked. "You worked hard in the office all day."

"Oh, it was nothing. I did some basic sketches at lunchtime, then finished while you guys obviously worked hard painting this evening. It's really shaping up," she said, scanning the freshly painted walls. She continued to outline her thoughts on decorating the rooms.

Jimbo was nearly speechless. When he gathered his thoughts, he took out his wallet and handed her a credit card. "Okay, Miss Mamie. What you have outlined sounds great. You just take this and do the shoppin' at Sears. You know Sears has everything The Company Store doesn't carry. If Randy trusts you with his office doin's, then I'll trust you to take care of all those details and do everythin' just the way you said. I have a deadline, and there is no way I can do all this alone."

"I'm glad to help. You can trust me. There is another thing I want you to trust me with. Come to the kitchen, sit down, and I am going to cut your hair. My mama cut my daddy's hair, and she taught me how. I know there isn't a barber close by who is open evenings, and you run the store all day. Come on. Please. Let me do this for you."

"Don't make it too short. I'm not in the Navy anymore, ya know."

Randy sat watching and listening while Jimbo got a haircut. Mamie also offered to spend Saturday weeding the flowerbeds and also borrow her brother's pressure washer to clean the porches, front and back.

Jimbo objected but not strongly. "I can't let you do all that, Mamie."

"Yes, you can. You need to let people help you. We all loved Miz Emma, and this is my way of honoring her. She loved this old house so much. After spending time in here the last two evenings, I can see why. You think of this house as a burden. It's not. It's a pleasure to spend time under this roof in these rooms, admiring a loving home to one of the nicest families in the area. Please, let me do what I can."

"Oh okay. I'm sure my sister and brother will appreciate the house lookin' good. I have some plans of my own. Whatever you can do will free up time for me to do the projects I can do."

"It's a deal then. See you early Saturday morning before it gets too hot. I'll bring some lemonade. It might be better for you than drinking all that coffee!" She gave him a smile that warmed him clear down to his toes.

He found himself smiling back, which felt good after so much unhappiness since Ma took sick and died and then Carol went back to Virginia and left him all alone in that huge empty house.

Randy was pleased with Jimbo's acceptance of help. He looked so much better with the haircut, eliminating the look of a mop on his head. "Are you finished, Mamie? It's getting late and we have another busy day at the office tomorrow, and Jimbo has a business to run. See ya, mate. Get some rest. Tomorrow is just minutes away."

"I don't know how to thank you guys. I am truly grateful."

When Mamie asked her brother to borrow his pressure washer, he asked, "Whatcha doing, sis?" When she explained, he volunteered to go along and help. "I looked up to Jimbo Webster all through school. He was only a few years older and set a good example of how a guy was supposed to behave. He's a good dude. Sure, sis, you can count on me."

Mamie and her brother showed up seven thirty Saturday morning. Even with a few breaks for lemonade, by lunchtime, the house was looking cared for once more. Jim did some of his own projects, going back and forth to check on the workers at the store. He brought back a flat of petunias Mamie asked for and rope for the porch swing to replace the rusty chain. They quit for lunch, and Jimbo did some hot dogs on the grill. Satisfied on a job well done, they agreed cooperation and helping hands made the job much easier. Mamie went to town to do the shopping for bedroom decorations and promised to spend as long as it took during the evenings next week to get the house in order before Carol and Robbie came home.

13

GETTING TOGETHER

Thursday morning, July 16, Carol was pleased with good weather that would enable her to fly to Lucerne with her brother. She dropped Susie off at her job as a summer camp counselor and followed Rob's directions as she drove her aging white Toyota Camry the short distance from Vienna, Virginia, to Dulles Airport, exiting for general aviation.

She saw Rob's black Mercedes at the pull off just past the exit. She flashed her lights. He pulled out and led her around to the general aviation side of the airport, stopping next to his private hangar. He pushed a remote-control button, and huge doors slid open, revealing his gleaming Bonanza looking fast just sitting there. Rob unlocked cockpit and cargo doors so they could each put a small suitcase in the baggage compartment, then he proceeded to do a preflight inspection as she followed him around the perimeter of the plane.

While Rob checked the airplane, Carol checked out Rob. He had on his usual dress pants, polo shirt, and Justin boots. She asked him once why he always looked dressed up. His answer made sense. "Ever since leaving the farm, I made myself a promise to never wear denim again. I hated the feel of denim on my skin, how it made me sweat and was so binding. I like the smoothness, the richness of a fine gabardine or imported wool." For casual dress, he usually wore topsiders but switched to Justin boots when flying. *Dashing* was certainly a good word to describe him, even though his athletic build had gone a little soft after all the years of easy living.

Rob drained a small amount of fuel out of each wing tank into a clear plastic tube to check for water and sediment. He uncovered the pitot tube, checked under the cowling for anything amiss, and checked oil, checked tires, wiggled ailerons and rudder, and checked hinge points on the flaps. Only then did he pull the plane out of the hangar with a hook inserted into a nose-wheel bracket. They each drove their car into the hangar, and Rob closed and locked the door.

He climbed up on the right wing, and she followed after he got into the left seat. She lowered herself into the right seat next to him. Rob reached across her to close and lock the door and checked her seatbelt being fastened properly. She knew the routine since this wasn't the first time she flew with Rob, but it was the first time in this new airplane.

No matter what anyone said about him, he was a thorough and good pilot. Rob handed her a headset for easier communication in the noisy environment; but she knew to keep quiet until he received all his clearances from ground control, tower, and departure control. They taxied a long way to stop before entering the active runway. Rob held the toe brakes; used the throttle to apply enough power to read 2,500 on the rpm gauge; and did his run-up to check the engine, propeller controls, and gauges; and set the magnetic compass.

When satisfied that all was in order, he asked for and was given takeoff clearance. He kept the plane going straight down a long, wide runway until the plane lifted off. Rob reached over, retracted the landing gear with a little wheel-looking lever, and then raised the flaps. They climbed smoothly into the clear blue Virginia sky, leveling off at 6,500 feet to get over mountain ridges. The flight would only take them an hour—a whole lot better than six hours of highway driving or flying into Pittsburgh, renting a car, and still have an hour's drive to Lucerne.

She heard Rob's acknowledgment of the control tower handing him over to departure control, then a courteous "Good day" as they left controlled airspace.

Carol finally relaxed and spoke for the first time since getting into the plane. "I really appreciate the convenience and cost saving of this trip. Please let me help with fuel cost."

"Don't worry about it, sis. Gives me a chance to show those narrow-minded people what can happen when you get out of a small town and go big. It will be worth it to see the looks on their faces. Keep your money and help your girls get an education. I was going anyway."

While they enjoyed the scenery from this altitude, Carol asked Rob, "How do you think Jimbo is handling life? I heard a few disturbing statements from him when we were home for Ma's funeral, which might indicate depression."

Rob glanced at her and patted her on the knee, "Don't worry about Jimbo. He may be a little short on intelligence, but he is harmless. Guys talk that way. He just wanted attention when he said, 'Life isn't worth living.' If you baby the guy, he will just play on your conscience. He'll get over whatever is bugging him. He needs to do what we did—get out of Lucerne. That place will drag anyone into bouts of depression. Actually, when you think about it, what kind of future does he actually have? Running that store isn't my idea of a career."

Carol thought a bit about what he said. "I suppose you are correct. I am concerned about him, though, being alone. He doesn't seem to have friends. I think he covers up his drinking. I wonder what he does when we aren't there."

"You worry too much. He's a big boy. He'll be fine," was Rob's response as he scanned the sky for any other traffic enjoying the beautiful weather.

She turned to her own thoughts of how to help Jimbo without moving back to Lucerne. Other than last evening, she only called him once since Ma's funeral when she let him know she arrived home safely. She could call him more often. She could have him visit her in Vienna and let him see another way of living. He could stay awhile since the house would be too empty without her daughters living at home.

The flight seemed too short as they rolled smoothly onto the runway at the new airport on the outskirts of Lucerne instead of going to Jimmy Stewart Field in Indiana, Pennsylvania. They taxied a short distance to an attractive blue-and-cream Morton hangar with one end used as a terminal. An attendant led them to the tie-down area then helped Rob push the Bonanza into position against the fence. They securely tied the plane down before the attendant brought a fuel truck over to top off the fuel tanks.

Rob was surprised when little brother Jimbo came out of the terminal to give them a ride into town. "Carol called me last night to let me know when you would be here. No need to rent a car. You can use Ma's Ford Fusion while you are here. Randy told me to take good care of it until the will was read and estate settled. I still have my old Bronco. Not the most comfortable car, but it takes me where I want to go." Not only was Jimbo clean-shaven, with shorter hair since they last saw him at the funeral, his dark eyes weren't hollow and bloodshot. Rob shook his hand with a "Good to see you, little brother, and I sincerely mean that."

Carol stood on tiptoes to hug him and didn't cringe at his odor. Someone must have said something to him. He was well dressed in gray slacks and a yellow shirt that set off his dark, good looks. He looked more like the Webster side than either Rob or Carol, both of whom had fair complexions like their mother's Smith side.

Jimbo carried both their suitcases and put them in Ma's trunk. When they arrived at the family home, the lawn was mowed, the porch swing looked as though it had been painted, and the rusty chain had been replaced with clean white ropes secured with intricate knots. The rambling rose was in bloom, and flowerbeds were weeded. The inside of the house smelled fresh, with no dust on coffee and end tables, and no stale cigarette smoke lingered.

Carol excused herself to take her bag upstairs to her childhood room and found a bouquet of flowers on the dresser and a clean fresh bed with one of Ma's handmade quilts as the spread that matched drapes and walls. She wondered if the walls had been painted. "Someone has definitely said something to Jimbo," she remarked to Rob who was out in the hall.

Rob had the same experience when he went into his childhood room. Either Jimbo hired someone to clean up or there were signs of their little brother finally taking life seriously. He peeked into Jimbo's room. Guitar posters were off the walls, and he finally changed from his ancient Star Wars bedspread. A soothing plaid spread in beige and blue covered his bed with matching window curtains, and a fresh coat of soft blue paint covered the walls. Rob peeked into his mother's room, and it was as though she were still there. He turned to Carol and said, "Perhaps we should take time to go through Ma's things while we have a little extra time."

Jimbo called from the kitchen, "Lunch is ready." They enjoyed a delicious chicken salad spread on crescents. True, the cherry pie was from the local Kroger, but it was tasty with a scoop of ice cream. A lively conversation was easy over lunch, and the three of them spent the afternoon talking about their personal lives and how difficult it was to come home without Ma being there. They made plans to go through her desk tomorrow morning before going to hear her will read.

Carol took a walk around town but wore a big hat of Ma's to keep people from recognizing her. Although people were kind to her at the funeral, she didn't know if they were being authentic. They ordered take out from a new deli for their supper, preferring to stay home. The swing on the back porch served as a casual spot to continue friendly conversation. She noticed the large backyard was mowed and trimmed. The garage was cleaned out. It looked as though the fields of hay had been harvested. Carol was feeling nostalgic. She wondered, *Where exactly is my home?*

While they were sitting there watching fireflies float against a darkening sky, like airborne flickering candles, a soft mewing noise came from the shadows. Carol slipped off the swing and found a tiny calico kitten hiding in a corner of the porch. "Ah, I think she is hungry, guys."

"Don't be givin' me any more work to do around here, Carol. Once you feed a cat, they stick around," Jimbo growled. "Nothing worse than a cat windin' 'round your legs when you are tryin' to get somethin' done."

However, Carol was already in the house getting a bowl and some milk and didn't hear a word he said. "You are such a sweet thing. Your fur is so soft, and the color of a newly minted penny. Where is your mama? Where are you from? How did you get here?" Carol crooned to the kitten before putting her down on a bed of old towels in the corner of the porch. The kitten lapped at the milk then curled up to sleep on the towels. The siblings chatted a bit more before heading off to bed. Carol's observation of Jimbo's mood eased her mind, but she decided to still keep an eye on him for the remainder of the visit.

Friday was cloudy, a good day to go through Ma's desk and room and decide what to do with everything. In the nightstand drawer was a notebook, which held a list of her treasured items and included a note: "Everything not on this list is labeled on the bottom or back for which of you is to take possession. Carol, my jewelry box is yours to share with your girls." There was also a list of what was valuable and what should be donated to Goodwill or Salvation Army if they didn't want it.

Carol commented, "Ma must have known her time was short. Everything is in order." They had no disagreements, and the morning's work was handled efficiently. Since Jimbo still lived in the house, Rob and Carol packed only one box each, labeled with their names, to be taken back in the airplane. The bulk would stay where it was as long as Jimbo was going to still live there. The reading of the will would answer some important questions. They would wait to see what else needed to be done.

Rob wandered into the upstairs library room and selected a few of his dad's books. "Hey, guys. Do you mind if I take a few of Dad's books? I know Ma donated some to the new town library, but there are still a lot on the shelves."

Neither one minded. Carol joined him in the room and sat down in her dad's reading chair next to the window. "I always felt this room was special for some reason. Ma avoided coming in here except to dust and vacuum. She had me clean in here when I was home. She always read somewhere else. I wonder why?"

"Maybe they needed their own space," he answered.

Anytime they went out on the back porch, the calico kitten was still there as Jimbo feared. After it consumed another bowlful of milk, Carol picked it up and sat on the swing for a long time, petting the kitten and thinking. She looked at her brothers. "I am going to name her Penny, since Penny's from heaven." To the kitten, she whispered, "Don't worry about Jimbo. He needs someone to love."

14

THE READING

Randy was happy he chose to have the reading of Miz Emma's will on a Saturday, which promised to be a beautiful day. A lot of town folk were at the lake or at Little League games. He asked his personal secretary Mamie to be present. Randy looked up from his desk as Mamie announced the Webster family had arrived.

    He stood to welcome them and was nearly bowled over by Carol's beauty and graceful movements. He knew she and Rob arrived on the sixteenth and thought he saw her yesterday from across the street when she was walking. A large hat made him unsure. Up close and personal was a different matter. She was dressed in a black pantsuit with a soft silver top and a simple strand of pearls he recognized as the ones Miz Emma constantly wore. Carol was even more beautiful than he remembered. The maturing years complimented her.

    Rob was the same boastful jerk he always was. Barely inside the door, he let Randy know he and Carol arrived in his Bonanza and parked next to a little Cherokee 140. Randy knew the Cherokee was probably his. Rob's blue silk Hawaiian shirt, while attractive, seemed out of place for the seriousness of today's event; and he bragged about being jet-lagged from his recent vacation in France.

    Jimbo was the surprise of the day. He was clear-eyed, clean-shaven, his clean hair combed neatly although still a little too long. He wore a navy-blue suit, soft blue shirt, and red-white-and-blue-striped tie he must have bought for Miz Emma's funeral. Jimbo held

Carol's chair for her as she gracefully sat. Mamie entered last and sat discreetly in the back of the room in case her services were needed. When Carol coughed, Mamie quietly provided a bottle of water.

When all were properly greeted and seated, Randy cleared his throat and tried to keep his eyes from straying back to Carol. He scanned each of them, trying to interpret their body language. Rob seemed nervous and acted as though he were already bored with the proceedings when nothing happened yet. Jimbo was attentive and courteous, something he hadn't seen in him for a long time. Carol was stunning. He yearned to find out more about her current situation and would try after business matters were completed. Finally, he asked, "Are you ready to hear your mother's final wishes?"

Carol nodded without any comment. Rob made a gesture to get rolling, "Let's get on with it so we can fly back to Virginia before this unpredictable weather closes in."

Jimbo sat on the edge of his chair and said, "Whenever you are ready, Randall" in the deepest voice he could muster in the presence of his older siblings. Carol smiled at Jimbo and gently touched his arm in a gesture of affection. Jimbo responded with a smile.

Randy began, "As you know, I have called you here to Lucerne to read your mother's will. There are business dealings of which you are unaware. As Lucerne changed after the mines shut down and miners moved away or died, many support businesses needed for miners and their families closed down when people went in search of other jobs. Children of miners were happy to not feel the pressure of following previous generations of men into underground tunnels. Property owners were willing to sell for whatever they could get so they could leave for greener pastures. Real estate prices dropped to pennies on the dollar. Since your mother did not spend much of the money your parents were awarded from his lawsuit against the coal company over his illness which led to his premature death as the result of black lung—"

"Whoa, hold it right there, Mr. Small-Town Lawyer," interrupted Rob as he stood and leaned menacingly on Randy's desk. "Back the boat up. What lawsuit? What award? How much are you talking about?"

Randy focused on Carol, ignoring Rob for a moment to calm old resentments trying to surface. "I suppose an explanation is in order since you seem to not know anything about my last statement." Glaring directly at Rob, he explained, "I may be a lawyer in a small town, as you say. However, for your information, I have represented many miners and their families in wrongful-death lawsuits. My staff and I used information substantiated and made public by others that the BNP Coal Company knew of a long list of mining hazards. Solving the problems would have been more costly than settlements they expected to pay.

"Many miners or their survivors were awarded large sums. Your father and mother asked me to help with the investment of his $9.4 million settlement, wisely investing nearly all of the money, only putting enough in their bank account to keep the house in repair and a few personal comforts. He was too sick to care, needed no money other than for his health care, and Miners' Health Care Benefit took care of him practically free. He didn't live much longer after an out-of-court agreement was reached since the coal company knew we had them over a barrel.

"As properties became available, Miz Emma called me and gave me authority to buy on her behalf in the name of her corporation. At the time of her passing, she owned most of Lucerne, including The Company Store and this building when my landlord wanted to sell. She was quite the powerhouse, running her Jaroc Enterprises. The name was derived from your three names: *Ja* for James, *Ro* for Robert, and *C* for Carol."

Randy looked at each one of them, who sat there with looks of disbelief on their faces. He never before saw Rob speechless, his head thrown back, looking at the ceiling fan going round and round. Jimbo's eyes were closed, and he was shaking his head mumbling, "No, no, no," nearly inaudibly. Finally opening his eyes, he conceded, "I thought Ma was havin' lunch with church ladies or gettin' her hair done. Was she really overseein' property investments? She was my landlady and never said a word?" Carol covered her mouth with her left, ringless hand, and her tears streamed, making her blue eyes more brilliant. Mamie handed her a box of tissues.

Carol composed herself and quietly asked, "What does this mean, Randy? What are we supposed to do with all this property? Jimbo is the only one who lives here. Rob and I have homes and jobs. And… I have too many questions, yet I am at a loss for words!"

Randy took advantage of their shock to say, "The answers you are seeking are included in your mother's will, which I haven't read yet. May I continue?"

All three simply nodded in agreement, and he began to read, "I, Emma Mae Smith Webster, being of sound mind, hereby bequeath to my surviving offspring, in equal shares, all my worldly goods. If one should abandon their share, the others have the option of buying his or her share. Paperwork has been initiated to turn the family home into a bed-and-breakfast in hopes Carol will return to run it with her brother, James."

Scanning their faces once more, Randy could see mental wheels turning, each off on their own calculations of what all of this meant. Randy continued reading, "James, my son, you have been running The Company Store on Main Street, not understanding I have owned that store for a few years. The store is now yours—lock, stock, and barrel.

"Robert, I have kept enough assets liquid, so your portion is readily available in order for you to continue your job as a pilot. There is no need to liquidate anything. Go on with your exciting life with my blessings.

"Carol, you had the right to leave town and raise your family. But it is time to come home. There are people here who love you." As those words were said, Randy looked directly at Carol with deep meaning in his eyes and a quick nod, which she seemed to understand and gave him a demure smile, abandoning for a moment her look of a deer caught in headlights.

Randy continued, "A full listing of properties, rental agreements, and plans for the town as it moves forward in its new life are on record with Randall and in notebooks in my office. He is instructed to assist each of you as he assisted your father and me so well in the past. Since you are hearing these words, I am no longer available for explanations. If you have any questions, please ask Randall.

"'With all my love as only a mother can give, I ask you to be good to each other. If possible, I will be watching your developments from wherever God chooses to send me.' Signed December 30, 2013, Emma Mae Smith Webster. There was an update filed shortly before her passing. There is more standard legal verbiage, but that ends the personal statement she wanted you to hear."

Randy lowered his eyes for a moment, took a sip of water, and then asked authoritatively, "Are there any questions?" He was greeted with blank stares of a stunned family. They were processing that their mother kept secrets. He could see they each knew they should have been more cognizant of what was going on in their parents' lives, especially their mother's. Even Jimbo didn't know about all these developments, and he was living in the same house while most of this was happening.

Randy was greeted with silence. "Since there are no questions at this time, I have been instructed to take you to your mother's office so you can see for yourselves where she spent many hours these last few years. You may have questions as you proceed through learning about and understanding the holdings here in Lucerne. Feel free to call on me anytime."

They all went to the lobby where a discreet door opened into a tiny elevator. Randy pressed the number 2 button. Slowly, they rose to a second floor where the door slid open to an unassuming hallway with only two doors, one labeled JAROC ENTERPRISES INC. Underneath, in very small letters, was *E. M. Webster*. Randy opened the door with a silver key edged in blue he produced from his pocket, one Carol remembered seeing on his desk while he read Ma's will.

Entering respectfully, Carol walked around behind the desk to a bookcase on top of a credenza against the wall behind a simple office chair. There were the notebooks Ma mentioned in her will, each one labeled with the name of a business she recognized from her walk around town and arranged alphabetically. She selected one which was labeled *Bloomers*. In her mother's neat handwriting were documents with the date the building was purchased, renovations done for new occupancy permit, rental agreement, and Bloomers' record of rent payments. There were several shelves full of notebooks containing, she assumed, the same information about other holdings.

Rob spouted off to Randy, "Ma couldn't have done all that," sweeping his hand to indicate the notebooks.

Jimbo stood up to Rob for his mother's abilities. "You weren't around. She went to adult education classes at the high school and then at Westmoreland Community College. She was always readin' and spent a lot of time on her computer at her desk in her bedroom. I must admit, I thought she was playin' Solitaire or emailin' friends. I believe you now, Randy." With a head nod toward Rob, he added, "There are none so blind as those who won't see."

Mamie entered the room holding three manila envelopes and handed one to each sibling. They found inside a list of properties owned by Miz Emma. There was no question their mother knew what she was doing. The evidence was impossible to ignore. Jimbo said with his head lowered, "Hard to tell what she could have accomplished if pancreatic cancer hadn't ended her life so quickly."

Randy added, "I have made reservations for six thirty for all of us to have dinner this evening at The Point, a new restaurant out at the lake. Mamie and I will answer any further questions you may have after you have time to think this over this afternoon."

15

THE REALIZATION

The three siblings left their mother's office and barely spoke a word. Randy locked the door and held out the key. No one moved to accept the key until Randy reached out to Carol, took her hand, and placed the key in her palm, curling her fingers around it. She looked at him with a bewildered expression.

Rob asked, "Do I need to stay any longer? I still have another two weeks of vacation left. I have plans."

Jimbo turned his back and punched the number 1 elevator button a little harder than necessary. They descended to the first floor in silence. Their shock was still too fresh.

As they exited the elevator downstairs, Randy asked Carol if she could stay a moment longer and he would take her home later. "Not right now, Randy. This is very upsetting news. I am feeling guilty about neglecting my mother and my brother. I was so wrapped up in my own life, I had no idea about any of this. Why don't you come by and pick us up at six for dinner after my brothers and I have time to talk about all we learned? We can talk more during dinner at The Point. Thank you so much for arranging that. I am sure my brothers and I will have more questions for you after we talk."

"All right, Carol. See you later. I am here for you whenever you need me," Randy said. "Oh and by the way, the town doesn't care about the past. Everyone is looking at a rosy future for Lucerne, with credit going to your mother. She got the ball rolling, and others are helping with the progression."

The three siblings took the information Randy provided and walked around town. Building after building after building belonged to their mother's corporation. Each property was either occupied, being restored, or property cleared of tumbledown houses.

New buildings were sprouting up. There was a new small library and a new elementary school since families were moving back to the peaceful country-styled town. With families moving in, so were some fast-food restaurants and the new higher-quality The Point restaurant where they would be going for dinner with Randy this evening. Rob was unusually quiet. Jimbo asked them all to stop in at the new coffee shop, and he paid for lattes for all. He spent a few extra minutes talking to the attractive barista.

When they sat down at an outdoor café table, Jimbo looked earnestly at Rob and Carol. "Guys, I have a rather simple request. I am tired of being called Jimbo. Do you two think you could bring yourselves to call me Jim? I got used to the name in the Navy, and I feel Jimbo is rather childish for a guy who is part owner of this town."

"Sure, *Jim*, welcome to adulthood," quipped Carol.

"I don't know, pal, but I'll try," stated Rob. "A habit that old is hard to break. I don't think that will be as hard as understanding we own most of this town." They talked about a few inconsequential topics, still too stunned to get down to details.

During the conversation, Rob again brought up that he wanted to get back to his vacation. Carol agreed to go back to their homes in the morning and promised to get together with Jim by phone in three days after coming to terms with this new development. They made a list of questions for Randy to answer at dinner.

Carol called Randy later to say Rob would drive them to the restaurant in Ma's Ford. After a late lunch, they sat at the dining room table with the documents spread out in front of them, each one quietly trying to understand all the documents and lists of properties. As they compared notes and asked questions, Carol added to the list of questions to be addressed with Randy.

16

DINNER AT THE POINT

When Rob came down from upstairs to go to dinner still dressed in his Hawaiian shirt, Carol convinced him to change into a suit and tie. "This is Pennsylvania, Rob. I understand that shirt is formal attire in Hawaii, but please." Jim wore his suit again; and Carol wore a cream-colored dress, short-heeled pumps, and still had on her mother's pearls.

At the restaurant, they were surprised to see Mamie with Randy. They presented the initial list of questions to Randy as soon as they sat down. He went over each question individually and provided as much detail as he could in a public place, giving them information on where to look to find desired details. "When you have time to fully digest the information in the envelopes you received this morning, I believe you will have a full understanding of your holdings and depth of love your mother felt for each of you and this town. Whatever you don't understand, feel free to call me. Jimbo—"

"Little brother doesn't like being called Jimbo anymore. Wants to be called Jim," Rob cut him off.

Glaring at Rob and speaking between gritted teeth, he said, "Okay, Jim. As I was about to say before being interrupted, you can stop by the office anytime. Mamie can help you understand. Won't you, Mamie?"

"Yes, I would be pleased to help answer your questions. Call me anytime," and she slipped a piece of paper to him containing her phone number. "You too, Robert or Carol." But she didn't slip her phone number to them.

Jim blushed. "Sure, I'll stop by soon. You did a fine job preparin' those reports. Rob, Carol, and I spent some time lookin' over the information." Turning to Randy, he added, "I don't think I have ever thanked you for your part in gettin' me back on track and helpin' with fixin' up the house. Thanks, Randy. I owe you one."

"I am available to you whenever you need me. That's what friends are for."

Randy reached out and patted Jim's shoulder. "I promised Miz Emma to watch over you as long as you are in Lucerne. I'll take that promise to my grave."

Dinner was pleasant, with Carol and Mamie sitting on either side of Randy with the brothers opposite. Some folks she knew from when she sang in church choir so long ago stopped by to say hello. She noticeably relaxed as the evening progressed. Rob kept them all entertained with his airline stories. Jim drank sparkling water and took note of attractive waitresses and grinned at Mamie. Too soon, they rose to go home. Randy took care of the check. Jim walked Mamie to her car to be sure she was safe and said, "I'll give you a call."

Randy walked Carol out to her mother's car, but then asked Carol to ride back to town with him. He said, "I want to get my extra key for the main door of my building—correction, *your* building—for you so you can go to your mother's upstairs office whenever you please. I may be in court or out of town when you want to visit." When they stopped in front of his house, he asked, "Would you like to come in for a nightcap?"

"I don't think that is wise. I need to get back to talk to my brothers some more before we leave town tomorrow morning." She stayed in his Volvo. He retrieved the key and drove her to the house she jointly owned with her brothers. The siblings did have a lot to talk about. Conversations over dinner plus contents of the envelopes revealed more of what their mother had been doing since their dad died.

17

CAROL

Carol stopped sighing about the time they reached the house that partially belonged to her. "Thank you, Randy, for all you have done to look after Ma, and also Jim. Although I talked with Ma often, she mainly asked what I was doing. I neglected to find out what she did other than her church activities and her problems with Jimbo—oops, Jim. That is going to be a hard habit to break. He is right. Since he has made an effort to change his ways, we need to start treating him more as an adult and less like little brother."

"You should have seen him just a few weeks ago. He let himself go even more after Miz Emma passed. He was in bad shape when I hand delivered his letter about reading the will. I was afraid he would toss it out without reading it if I didn't take the letter to him personally," Randy replied. "I guess my constant little doses of tough love finally paid off. He has made a huge step toward recovery. I hope it lasts. If you could visit more often, I know he would appreciate it. Miz Emma tried, but he probably resented her mothering at his age and after being away for four years. As you said, he is an adult now. I know he was hurt by not being able to come back for your dad's funeral since his ship was out to sea on maneuvers. Give him some support and some time. I think he is over the hardest part."

"I was shocked at his deterioration during Ma's illness and death. I am relieved he has a new outlook on life. I hope he holds up over the new responsibilities ahead. Meanwhile, Rob and I plan to leave in the morning to go back to our homes in Virginia. We'll see how the future develops. Ma's will has given me a lot to think about. I do promise to stay better in touch with, ah, Jim. And you let me know what I can do to relieve you of the management of Ma's affairs. Okay?"

"Yes, Carol. Let's talk by phone after you have a chance to talk to your brothers to see how you are going to run this business opportunity your mother left you three. I will happily draw up whatever agreements you want." Randy reached over and took her hand, shaking it thoughtfully.

Carol thought he wasn't going to let go. She felt the handshake could have turned into something else. She withdrew her hand, turned quickly, and said, "Goodbye. See ya later, alligator," as he started to get out to open the door for her. Chivalry wasn't completely dead after all.

She walked into the house, and her brothers were sitting in the living room sharing a few beers by the looks of empties on the coffee table.

"Hey, sis," called Rob. "Come join us."

"Sure, but make mine a Sprite," she answered.

"What do you think about this sticky mess we are in?" asked Rob. "I thought I was out of this town. Looks like I am a property owner here whether I like it or not. Want to buy me out? Either of you?"

Jim looked back and forth between the two of them, waiting for someone to speak. He finally spoke up, "I never took Ma seriously. She got dressed up most days and went somewhere. I thought it was her church interests. Turns out she was buyin' the town. Now I own the store and the contents. She wants me to open the house as a bed-and-breakfast. How am I supposed to do all this on my own? You two will leave tomorrow and leave me to deal with all this. That's not fair, you know? Not. Fair. I am goin' to bed. I'll be up early to make some breakfast and drive you to the airport. G'night. Sleep tight. Don't let the bedbugs bite." He reverted to an old saying from their childhood.

Rob and Carol sat in silence until they heard Jim's bedroom door click closed. "What do you think we should do, Robbie?" Carol quietly asked. "Jimbo can't handle all this on his own. You and I have established lives away from Lucerne. I don't want to come back any more than you do, but I don't see Jimbo handling everything. The stress will hamper his recovery. He is too vulnerable. He needs support. Like it or not, we have a responsibility to at least look into continuing Ma's plan."

Rob shrugged and ignored her while he lazily read the matchbook covers in the crystal bowl on the coffee table. "Did Grammie Smith keep candy in this crystal bowl? I wouldn't mind having that unless you want it?"

Carol wasn't surprised when Rob didn't want to talk about their situation. "You can have it as far as I'm concerned, but check with Jim. You boys were the ones who went straight to the candy bowl when we visited Grammie." Carol took her bottle of Sprite and wandered through the house and out to the back porch. The kitten was still there. She took Penny into the kitchen for a bowlful of milk and some Purina kitten chow she picked up earlier on her walk around town.

Rob heard her in the kitchen, took the empty bottles to the recycle bin, and looked at her with a pained expression before responding, "Don't think any of this means a rat's ass to me. However, I am shocked at the new person Jim has become. I tested him this evening to see if I could get him drunk while you were out lollygagging with your pal, Randy. Jim barely sipped his beer. Those empties were mine, but I can handle it. I was serious when I said I want one of you to buy me out. I don't want to be any part of Ma's plans. I am not coming back to Lucerne and get swallowed up by misery."

Carol put the kitten back out on the porch, turned to Rob, and declared, "I need time to think, and you need to come up with what you feel a proper settlement would be. In order to determine what your one third is, we will need estimates or appraisals of all properties and balances in investment accounts. I will consider it, but I need more information before I can say anything more. Randy has been paying utility bills and handling everything for Ma. I will take care of getting the information from him that we need to make an informed decision. Yeah, I am going to bed too. Watch out for bedbugs," she called over her shoulder. "Alarm set for 0700, right?"

18

ROB

The soft morning light revealed lake-effect fog, a common situation in these valleys downwind from Lake Erie. In winter, there was snow and, in summer, blessed fog. He looked out the window and saw a low ceiling and limited visibility. He showered, shaved, dressed, packed his bag, and went downstairs since he heard soft voices and smelled coffee and another tantalizing aroma coming from the kitchen. When he entered the kitchen, he found his younger brother and sister. He felt as though he interrupted something when they grew silent.

Jim was holding Penny and petting the little stray as though she was his last friend. Rob sarcastically greeted them, "G'morning, you two. Lovely day out there, isn't it? Glad I am still on vacation and don't have to be home today. My plans start on Wednesday. How about you, sis? Can we delay until the fog burns off, or do I need to file an instrument flight plan?"

"I am in no hurry, Rob. I brought my computer along in case of delay. I work from home a lot, and Susie is at camp. I'll use this opportunity to visit Ma's office again if you don't mind. Do either of you want to come along?" Carol offered.

Both brothers simply shook their heads. Rob mumbled a "negative" before jamming his mouth full of pancakes and reaching for some thick bacon Jim fried earlier. When Rob was finished eating, he put his plate and utensils in the dishwasher, refilled his coffee mug, and went to the living room TV to watch the Weather Channel.

Jim put the kitten out the back door, went to the foyer closet for a light jacket, and excused himself. "I'm gonna check on the help at the store. Call me there when you are ready to do whatever you are gonna do. I'll drive you back to the airport. Leave the Ford here in the garage. I noticed the inspection sticker is about to expire anyway."

Carol joined Rob in the living room. The TV was on mute, so they were able to talk while Rob watched weather forecasts. "I'm going over to Ma's office to browse through the notebooks of properties owned by Jaroc. If Randy is available, I might have a chat with him too. I need more answers. I sat up half the night making a list of questions."

Rob wished her a good day. Then, he leaned back on the old comfortable sofa, propped his feet on the coffee table, nearly knocking the crystal bowl full of matchbooks onto the floor, and zoned out. He hadn't slept well either, but he did not care enough to make a list of questions. Each time he fell asleep, he was jolted awake by a nightmare about Randy and him playing football back at Lucerne High School. He really did not want to relive all the bad memories of living here. In no time at all, he was snoring with blue light from the TV flashing over the room, still on mute. He didn't notice the fog gradually dissipating outside the window.

19

AN AGREEMENT

As Jim parked his Bronco in the back lot of The Company Store and walked toward the old building that was now his, he was aware of a feeling of pride in being the owner. He walked a little taller and entered the door with a feeling of authority. He thought to himself, *I'm no longer just a worker here. This is mine. I can make changes and get more up-to-date stock.* Jim checked on the help and found the young boys busy restocking shelves. "Hey guys. Could you dust the shelves before restocking?"

They were surprised, but George said, "We can do that."

Since it was Sunday, they didn't open until one. He reflected back on another Sunday morning a few short weeks ago when he almost lost everything. Amazing how life changed in such a short time.

Concluding his business there, he took time for another stroll around town with a new perspective. When he saw Carol in Ma's white Ford Fusion parking in front of the law office a few minutes later, he caught up to her and asked, "May I join you, Carol? I don't want to butt in or anything, but I have questions."

"Sure, Jim," she answered with a smile. "Thanks for caring. I don't think Rob gives a hoot. Let's find out what is what. You are as much a part of this as I am, maybe more so since you live here."

Carol unlocked the outer door. They went in and she relocked the door from inside. Randy didn't respond to a knock on his office door, so Jim and Carol took the elevator to the second floor. She slipped the key Randy gave her into the lock and went into Ma's office. Carol noted a modern fax machine, computer, and Wi-Fi capability already in the office. She sat down in Ma's chair and took one row of notebooks off the credenza and arranged them on the desk in two piles. "You go through those," she said, pushing one stack toward Jim.

Jim was happy to be finally treated as an equal by Carol. He always looked up to his big sister, yet the age difference and distance made it difficult to feel close to her. He was still an adolescent when she left town, and she stayed away while raising her two children on her own. They didn't keep in touch well while he was away in the Navy; and, well, life had been complicated after he got back and moved in with Ma.

Jim broke the silence of their concentrating when he reported, "Ma was astute, Carol. Everything is in the corporation name. I believe that means we automatically inherit without any complication, although I will check with Randy's secretary to be sure."

Carol looked up from her stack of notebooks with a huge smile, noting his blush when Jim mentioned Mamie. "The will does state there are liquid assets for Rob. She knew, didn't she? What a woman! Jim, I spent considerable amount of time last night thinking about this situation when I should have been sleeping. I was going to call you after I got home. However, since you are here, I have a proposition for you."

Jim looked up with a puzzled expression, wondering what she was going to say.

Carol noted his reaction. "I am thinking, and this is just a thought for now. It's not definite yet, but I think I need to go home…"

Jim's shoulders slumped as he looked down at the floor then back at her with the saddest look she had seen since Uncle Otto had a beagle pup so long ago.

"Wait a minute, Jim. Let me finish. I need to go home, pack up, and come back here to help run Ma's holdings. We don't need to buy out Rob. He can have his one third share out of invested funds.

Good grief. There apparently is plenty to share if the balances are for real in statements I found last night. He can go on with his carefree life. We will co-own the properties. My rental house in Virginia is on a month-to-month basis. I doubt my daughters will be coming home to live with me again. There is room enough for now in our family home for their visits. I can help you, and you can help me. We can do this together, Jim, can't we? There is room to have horses for a riding stable with the B&B. You can teach fishing to tourists at the lake. There are so many opportunities coming to mind. I am actually getting excited about the many possibilities."

Jim's hangdog look gradually turned into a smile as she spoke. He and Carol both rose from their chairs to share a hug and handshake on their newly found joint adventure. Jim helped Carol carefully place the notebooks on the shelf as they were. "Carol, you don't know how much I appreciate your offer to come home. It has been rough around here. Ma was always on my back about my drinking and smoking. The more she harped, the worse I behaved. I am ashamed of myself. Since Ma died, I have been really lost. I miss my buddies from Navy days, and I miss discipline of military life. I didn't realize how messed up I was until Randy told me to get my act together. He knew. I think he cared a lot for Ma just as he cares a lot for you. I will be able to take care of things until you can go home and make moving arrangements. Could you come stay at the house and help get it ready to turn into the B&B of Ma's dreams? You can get your own place later. If you want, I will move into Gran's apartment over the garage."

"Jim, I can certainly do all that. I won't be under pressure to find a place right away. Maybe we already own a comfortable place for me to live and don't know," she stated, nodding toward the row of notebooks. "You don't need to move out of the house. That way, we can have more time to talk and plan the future. I need to talk with my daughters and explain why I want to give up the house they have always called home. There are a lot of bad memories there for me. I don't see why they would object since I raised them to be independent. They are about to leave the so-called nest. I don't see

Rob often enough to stay in the area for him. And little Penny needs another friend."

They left the office with a promise to return soon, shared a chuckle as they joined hands, and said in unison, "God bless you, Ma."

20

RANDY

Randy noted Rob's gleaming Bonanza 33 still parked beside his Cherokee 140 when he arrived at the airport on Sunday afternoon. The fog must have kept them from leaving instead of Rob filing an instrument flight plan to fly to Dulles. He was starting his preflight inspection when he heard tires crunching on gravel and saw Jim's old Bronco pull into the parking lot. The three siblings got out to walk toward the flight line with Jim carrying Carol's bag.

"Hi there," he called. "I am glad to see you waited for the fog to lift. You will still have some turbulence over the hills on your way back."

"I already called flight service for a full weather briefing, thank you. And I filed a flight plan in case we are lost in the mountains. Not my first flight, you know?" Rob ignored Randy and went straight to checking under the cowling.

When Carol got closer, she said, "Hello, Randy. Jim and I have news for you. I am coming back to town as soon as I can make moving arrangements. We can talk more later. However, here's our plan. When you have time, calculate the approximate value of Ma's estate. Rob is requesting his portion in cash. Jim and I plan to work together. I will help Jim get B&B approval and help run it and Ma's office, collecting rents and whatever else comes along. We have some ideas for expansion and will need some advice if you are willing to continue representing us as you so faithfully attended Dad and Ma.

Jim will continue operating The Company Store and will do maintenance on the house to keep it running smoothly. The house is big enough for us to share until I eventually find a place of my own. That's it in a nutshell. How does that sound?"

Randy tried to not show his excitement about Carol's announcement she would be moving back to Lucerne. "Sounds good, Carol. I think you have a workable plan. I know a lot of people will be happy to have you back in town." Randy smiled as he turned to finish his preflight walk around his airplane.

Rob interrupted his own preflight checklist to pull Randy aside behind their individual airplanes and reached out to shake hands. Rob looked him in the eye, "Thanks, Randy."

"Why are you thanking me?" Randy asked as he cautiously shook hands.

"Well, I was pretty pissed when you got that scholarship I wanted. However, if I had gotten it, none of this would be happening. I have to admit I have been a royal pain. I ignored my duties to my folks. I want to make amends. Don't distribute my portion of the estate until the B&B is up and running. I want to be a part of what happens, like a silent partner. If possible, put Ma's Fusion in Carol's name. The heap she is driving won't make the trip back here. And we never had this conversation. Understood?"

Randy nodded with a sly grin. "Gotcha."

The sun shone brightly as they each taxied to the runway, taking off into a clear blue sky. Randy headed to Kentucky for a trial starting Monday. Rob and Carol were headed toward their homes in the Virginia suburbs. Randy smiled the rest of the day. He knew he wanted Carol to live in his home—with him if she would have him. He knew he would have his work cut out for him, as Carol was a self-sufficient person not needing a man to complete her. However, he needed her.

21

CAROL

The flight to Virginia was a little bumpy over the hills as Randy said and Rob warned her. To keep her busy, Rob showed her how to hold the yoke steady as he checked charts, and she enjoyed time spent with him. When they arrived at Rob's hangar at Dulles Airport and exited his Bonanza, Rob's Mercedes quickly purred into action to back out of the hangar.

Carol's old Camry didn't want to start. She pleaded and coaxed, finally starting the old girl on the fifth try. She helped Rob put his Bonanza away, although there was little to do except watch wingtips. He attached a long steel cable to a tie-down ring on the tail and ran a motorized device by remote control to wrap the cable while he used a nosewheel hook to steer. Rob closed and locked the hangar door and gave her a goodbye hug. "If that old car of yours gives you any more problems, let me know, sis."

"Sure, Rob. Thanks again for the ride. Let's talk more about what part, if any, you want to have in the Lucerne developments. Call me after you have some time to come to a conclusion. I need to do some more research too." She got in her car and headed for Vienna and some personal decisions she needed to make. With her mind on her to-do list and events of the past few days, she wasn't aware of steam coming from under the Camry's hood until she heard a whistle and noticed the heat gauge was high. She pulled out of traffic to the side of the road and started to call Rob.

She watched in her rearview mirror as a green Ford pickup truck pulled off the highway and stopped behind her. Two men—respectfully dressed in clean jeans, polo shirts, and ball caps—walked up next to her car. She opened the window only a small crack to hear what they said.

"Ma'am, do you need help?" one of them asked. She looked from one to the other. They looked identical: tall, thin, piercing blue eyes, curly brown hair sticking out from under their ball caps. Concern showed on their faces. "Hello, ma'am. Are you okay? Do you need help?" the other one asked again while she sat there trying to decide what to do. Seeing her worried look, each one reached into a shirt pocket, producing business cards which they handed to her through the slit of opened window.

Carol took the business cards. Jacob Harrison owned Jacob's Automotive Repair Shop in Tyson's Corner, where she turned off Route 7 to go to her home in Vienna. She knew where that was. Jonathan Harrison's business address was Harrison's Construction Company in Williamstown, Pennsylvania, close to Lucerne. They were obviously twins or at least brothers. "How about that?" she said as she looked at them through the window. "I plan to move to Lucerne in a few weeks practically next to Williamstown. Small world, isn't it?"

"I am the one from Williamstown. Jonathan Harrison at your service, ma'am." He removed his cap, as would a knight, accompanied by a sweeping bow. "My brother and I were behind you and saw your car has a problem. What can we do to help? This isn't a safe place for an attractive young lady as yourself to be disabled."

"I'll pay you later for the compliment, sir. I don't know what the problem is. I'll have to call for a tow truck, or my brother lives not too far away. He can come to take me home to Vienna and deal with the car. I was just going to call him," she asserted, holding out her cell phone.

Jacob spoke, "Just so happens, ma'am, I own a tow truck. Why don't we take you home and then come back with my truck and take your car to my shop?" Holding up two fingers, he added, "Scouts honor, ma'am, we'll take good care of you and your car. Come on, let us do our good deed for the day."

Hesitantly, Carol introduced herself while she collected her purse. Jonathan got her bag and a small box of some of her mother's things from the back seat and helped her get settled into the club cab of Jacob's pickup after she locked her car. She gave them her address, directions to her house, and the Camry's keys to Jacob. After the short drive, Jonathan carried her bag to the front door of her house and waited until she unlocked and was safely inside. She gave Jacob her phone number to call her with an estimate on the car repair. He tipped his baseball cap and said he would be in touch soon. She uttered a prayer, "Lord, I hope these men are honest. I am finally seeing a brighter future ahead." So far, they did what they said they would do. *Such nice young men,* she thought.

She unpacked her bag and computer and started writing an article for this week's newspaper. When the phone rang about five thirty, she was surprised to see Jacob's business name on the caller ID. "Do you have good news, Mr. Harrison?"

"Please call me Jacob. I have good and bad news for you. The bad news is you have a blown head gasket. The good news, I can have it fixed by noon tomorrow. Do you need transportation anywhere this evening? I can take you a loaner." Jacob seemed truly apologetic.

"I am so busy this evening, I won't miss having a car. My neighbor can take me to your shop when the Camry is ready." Carol was worried about the repair bill. Although she owned part of her old hometown, her checking account was still short on funds.

"Oh don't worry. Jonathan and I will deliver your car. I'll call first to make sure you are home. See ya 'bout lunchtime."

"I'll be here. You have my car." Carol called Rob to let him know what happened, but she was home safely and her Camry would be fixed by tomorrow. He let her know he would help out if she needed a temporary loan. Promptly at noon the following day, Jacob called to say her car was repaired, then he and Jonathan delivered her car. "How much do I owe you?" she asked while opening her checkbook.

"Well, about that. I teach a class at Vienna Vocational Academy. I had a group of my senior students assist in the repair, getting some hands-on practice. Why don't we call it another good deed? I moved today's lesson plan to another day. Your car breaking down was an opportunity for my students. Oh, and one of the students said he would buy your Camry if you ever decide to sell," Jacob answered.

Carol looked at Jacob in disbelief, thanking her lucky stars for her good fortune in meeting these two men. Jacob handed her the car keys. Jonathan, who had been looking up at a loose section of siding on the front of the house, came up to her and said, "Looks like you need a little siding repair. Since that's my specialty, would you like me to come by later this evening to fix it for you? No charge?"

"I'm only renting. I have told my landlord about the loose siding, and he can't come to do the repair since he is stationed in Maine right now. I couldn't let you do the work for nothing. How about some hamburgers and potato salad on the porch? About six? I'm not known for my cooking, but no one ever complained."

"You have a deal," he answered eagerly. He really wanted to help her and to get to know Carol better. If she were moving to Lucerne, they would practically be neighbors. He whistled happily as he and Jacob drove back to the shop. He stopped by Lowe's and Kroger on the way to her house later in the evening. He showed up at her door with hammer, nails, some caulking, and a watermelon for dessert. The repairs were done at the same time the hamburgers came off the grill. He was a gentleman throughout the evening of small talk. He was able to tell her about some of the developments in the area she hoped to be moving to soon.

Over the next few days, she spent some extra time in the library's research room exploring the ins and outs of running a B&B. She visited a similar business on the outskirts of town, talking to the owner for an extensive time about the demanding schedule. Their conversation was interrupted several times by phone calls from people making reservations or asking questions about things to do in the area.

"All just part of the job. Sometimes, it is quiet, sometimes hectic. The best part is the people you meet. And the worst part is the people you meet," the owner said with a little chuckle. "About 95 percent of the people are wonderful. The other 5 percent are a challenge. But the customer is always right. And treat them with respect even when they are wrong. Just try to please as many people as you can. Some people enjoy being difficult. Thank goodness those people are few and far between."

Carol picked up several pamphlets to read at home. After a lot of back-and-forth thoughts, she was surer of her tentative decision to move back to Lucerne and start a new career in the old hometown. She still needed to let her girls know. She would be moving from the only home they had ever known. Although they were almost out on their own, they had their personal belongings to move. This could be quite heart wrenching for them.

22

FINAL DECISION

Susie came home on the weekend from her summer camp counselor position. Carol gave her details about events of the last few days. "While I was there for the reading of your grandmother's will, I learned my brother can't do everything necessary to keep Ma's business venture running. Susie, I have made a decision regarding the situation in Lucerne. How would you feel about spending the rest of your summer there?"

She saw Susie's expression change. Tears were glistening in her eyes as she turned away to wipe them dry. Carol quickly continued, "Did I tell you my brothers and I inherited quite a bit of money, as well as property? Did I tell you there is a kitten living on the porch? We talked about adding horses for a riding stable. I know you love horses, honey. You have always been fond of your Uncle Jimbo. By the way, we now call him Jim. You could go swimming at the lake. There is a lot to do. One of the advantages would be no more worry about how I will afford to pay for your schooling. You can follow your dream of becoming a veterinarian. I know you have a magical touch when it comes to caring for animals, and I'll let you get another dog. You miss having a dog since Cindy died."

"You mean it, Mom?" Susie asked after a long silence during which her expression changed from a tear-filled frown to a half smile. "I know how you scrimp and save to send Roberta to school. I don't want to put you through that for me. It takes extra years to become a vet. I will go along with whatever you decide. You seem enthused just talking about it. So sure, let's do it. What did you name the kitten?"

"I named her Penny due to her color, and we didn't know where she came from. I decided Penny must be from heaven, like an old song I used to sing. She's a calico and loves to be held."

"Is she allowed in the house? Or does Uncle Jimbo—ah, Jim—make her stay outside? How soon is this move going to take place?"

"Oh, she has already worked her way into Jim's heart. She'll steal yours too. Just you wait. But you won't have long to wait. Can you be ready by the end of the month?"

Roberta, always the emotional one, took it well over the phone. "Mom, you have taken such good care of us. Taking these summer courses mean I will have enough credits to graduate midyear. Wait until you hear this! My part-time job here in Winchester has been offered to me full time. I was going to call you this weekend to break the news to you that I won't be going back home after graduation. I like the staff. They must like me, or they wouldn't want me full time. Sure, Mom. I can get up to Lucerne to visit. I am happy for you. Wow, a B&B owner. Sounds cool."

"Well, I don't know how *cool* it will be. I'm sure there will be a lot of work to do before we are licensed. I have a lot to learn. When can you come to pack up your belongings? Soon, I hope. Now that the decision is final, I need to get back to Lucerne ASAP."

"How about this weekend? One of my friends is going home to see her mother. I can ride along."

Carol was relieved to have that phone call out of the way. The die was cast. She broke the news to her landlord, who complimented her on her prompt rent payments over the years. He wished her well and said a two-week notice was sufficient. He was due to retire from the Navy and would do some remodeling before he and his wife moved in.

On Wednesday, while submitting her article for this week's newspaper, Carol tried to give a two-week notice to the editor. Mr. Gardner asked, "Could you continue writing and submitting via the internet?"

She agreed to try for a while. Since she wasn't sure how involved she would be while running a B&B and Ma's office, she said she would continue as long as she could. The B&B clientele might give her more stories to tell. The librarian said she would be missed but wished her well in her new endeavor.

Carol spent time each day getting her belongings in order, selling a lot at a neighborhood garage sale. Since the house was furnished when she and Ted rented it, she was left with clothing, a few personal treasures she accumulated over the years, her files of her stories she wrote, and her office machines.

Jonathan Harrison surprised her with a phone call. After some small talk about the weather, he asked, "Have you decided whether or not you are moving to Lucerne, and if so, when?"

"After a lot of research and soul-searching, yes, I am moving the end of the month. I have been cleaning out and packing."

He offered, "I could help you move if you want. I flew down here to visit Jacob. He has given me some of his woodworking tools, a bedroom suite, and some other furniture that belonged to our parents. I don't need a whole truck for my things. Why don't I rent a U-Haul truck? We can help you load your belongings, and I'll drive it for you. How big of a truck do you estimate you'll need?"

"No big furniture to move, so I don't need much. Probably a little more than a pickup truck would be sufficient for me." Carol couldn't believe her good luck. First of all, he rescued her along Dulles Access Highway, then fixed the house, and was offering to help her move? There must be someone looking after her from above. All she could do was agree to his suggestion and say heartfelt thanks.

Roberta came for the weekend and took a few boxes of her belongings and asked her mom to store three other boxes for her in Lucerne until she had a permanent place to live. She was aglow over a new guy she met. Susie packed her belongings to add to the U-Haul move to Lucerne for two months before leaving for college.

Just before moving day, Rob called to ask if she would be home that evening. He had a surprise. She made fried rice to share with him and was shocked and pleased when he pulled in with Ma's white Ford Fusion. "I figured you needed the car now and took the airline jump seat back to Pittsburgh. Jim picked me up, I drove 'er back, and here she is. Randy took care of getting the title transferred to your name. She's all yours, sis. I will call for airport transportation to get back home. Something smells great. Oh yes, and here is something else Randy sent you." Rob handed her an envelope containing a new Pennsylvania registration for the car and a check for ten thousand dollars. "He said this is part of his duty as executor, and we each got a check as the first phase of settling the estate."

Carol's eyes filled with tears as she realized her financial worries might be over. Although there was a lot more to worry about, it seemed money could be taken off her list of worries keeping her awake at night. There in black and white was her name and address on the car's registration, already establishing her in her former home. She and Rob enjoyed a nice meal, and the airport van picked him up at her driveway. She called Jacob and told him his student could have the Camry for $250. It didn't owe her anything.

On July 30, Jonathan came with a U-Haul truck with Jacob following in his pickup. The two guys loaded Carol's and the daughters' meager belongings. Jonathan led the way to Pennsylvania while Carol and Susie followed in their Ford Fusion. They were headed into a new life.

PART 3

END OF JULY 2015 TO SPRING 2016

23

BACK IN LUCERNE

Jonathan helped Susie and Carol unload their belongings from the U-Haul truck into the appropriate rooms at the old family home in Lucerne. Carol followed Jonathan to Williamstown where she and a neighbor helped Jonathan unload his furniture. Although not fancy, his ranch house was in a good neighborhood and was well maintained.

When he returned the rental truck, she drove Jonathan back to his house. He could not have been more of a gentleman throughout the day. Although he said he would be in touch and for her to call him if she needed anything more, she didn't expect she would hear from him again. He was just one of those blessings to come her way when she needed an angel. They shook hands. Jonathan touched her elbow with a look on his face as though he wanted to say something more. However, he only muttered, "Nice to get to know ya."

"Same here. Thanks for all you did today, and the car repair, and… just for being a friend when I needed one." She got into her car and watched him in the rearview mirror watching her as she drove away. She wondered why he was watching but had greater things to worry about as she headed to Lucerne to reestablish into her former hometown.

Susie was nearly unpacked in Ma's old bedroom. Carol unpacked her clothing and headed for the kitchen to put some of her favorite pans away. Carol felt her mother's presence since Ma spent the majority of her time in the kitchen. Ma canned garden produce for good eating all year. When anyone dropped by to visit at mealtime, a normal thing for family and friends to do, Ma would send someone to the basement shelves to get a jar of corn, tomatoes, green beans, pickled beets, jelly, potatoes from the old coal bin, or whatever she needed to spread the meal over as many more family or friends were invited to stay and eat. No one ever left hungry.

Ma used to make homemade ketchup or tomato soup from juicy, ripe tomatoes. Cabbage went into huge crocks to make sauerkraut. Cucumbers became the best pickles on earth. Her nine-day pickles were processed through multiple salt brines until they were unbelievably crisp and tasty. Dill pickles were made with fresh dill from a patch at the garden's edge, and then a leaf from grape vines on the hill was packed in each jar.

Carol could almost smell Ma's homemade bread baking. Kneading bread dough helped relieve her stress of homemaking. Part of bread making would include cinnamon buns with nuts and brown sugar to make a bottom caramel coating.

Memories flooded back of picking wild blueberries (called huckleberries) or blackberries and walking home swinging buckets full of ripe berries. Ma made flaky, delicious pies from berries that survived being eaten right off the bushes from purpled fingers. She also made jellies and preserves, sealing tops of jars with melted paraffin wax. There was nothing better than a thick slab of homemade bread slathered with Ma's preserves.

Ma made everyone's favorite strawberry jam from fresh-picked strawberries from their own little patch next to the shed. Carol remembered gathering eggs from the chicken coop, now gone, and chasing free-range chickens back to safety in their coop before dark. Having all those fresh ingredients added to the tastiness, availability, and abundance of food served at mealtimes.

The black walnut tree in the backyard gave a real challenge to harvesting precious nutmeat. In addition, Carol recalled her Dad taking all of them nutting: traipsing around the countryside, picking up fallen nuts, taking them home, spending time cracking and picking, and putting jars full of nutmeat with the other canned food on shelves in the cool side of the basement until a freezer was purchased.

Over long winter evenings, Dad sat cracking nuts, doling out tidbits while Ma read from family-style books such as *Pollyanna*, *Heidi*, or the *Hardy Boys*.

Carol recalled Ma making fudge, cookies, date loaf, and homemade ice cream with peaches picked in Grandfather's orchard and canned. Ma frequently made cakes. She didn't need any help from Duncan Hines or Betty Crocker. No wonder flour and sugar were purchased in 20-pound bags.

Carol struggled to come back to reality to continue settling into her former home. Susie came downstairs to help, and Carol said, "I am the lady of the house now. I wonder if I'll ever be the cook my mother was? I promise you to follow Ma's favorite saying, 'Always finish what you start.' I'm not entirely sure what I am starting, but I will do my best to follow it to its conclusion, however or whatever that may be."

They both wandered into the living room to sit for a minute. Penny was curled up in a living room chair, no longer restricted to the back porch. Jim came home from The Company Store, picked up the growing kitten, and took her to the kitchen to feed her. Then, Carol, Susie, and Jim ate the pizza he brought home. They spent the evening making plans and notes at the dining room table while Susie washed dishes before joining them. Susie held Penny, getting acquainted with the soft bundle of fur.

Early next morning, Carol took some file boxes over to Ma's office. Randy, on his way to church, saw her pull to the curb. He stopped to welcome her back to Lucerne. "Is there anything I can do to help?" he asked.

Carol greeted him with a warm smile. "Thanks for the distribution of estate funds. Sure helped with my move." She added, "By the way, I need the building inspector's name and number. I want to start on the B&B application while Jim is willing to get the work done. We talked and made plans, but we want to see what is involved before we start preparations."

"Good idea. Sure, I will call Alex Graham on your behalf and let him know you are moving forward on the application Miz Emma already filed. Expect a call from him next week. Would you have lunch with me on Monday so I can go over a few more details?"

"Sure, I still have questions. I wish I knew more about what Ma had in mind. I am still overwhelmed with the idea of picking up where she left off. However, she left plenty of information. I just need to do more reading of her notebooks."

Randy helped Carol carry boxes from her car to the elevator and into the upstairs office. "You look so natural working here in your mother's office. You'll soon feel as though you belong. Give yourself time to settle in. You'll be okay. Would you like to go to church with me today? I plan to spend an hour downstairs in my office before leaving, if that will give you enough time to unpack."

She felt badly for refusing. "Not today. I have too much to do. Maybe some time." She announced, never lifting her eyes from boxes she was unpacking. Randy left, smiling as he quietly closed her door. She placed photos of her daughters on the desk, moving Ma's photos onto the credenza. She spent the rest of the day getting settled. She created a spreadsheet on Excel of rental properties, addresses, contact information, amount of rent, due date, and date paid, and printed it out so she could keep one at the house for Jim's review. She made a list of things to do for the coming week. She sent an email to Randy, asking for additional copies of Ma's death certificate so she could make necessary changes to bank accounts and post office box. By suppertime, she felt comfortable with everything she accomplished.

When Jim got home from work on Sunday evening, he told Carol, "It's going to be good having you and Susie in the house again. It was too big of a house for just me. I never got used to living alone since I went from living at home to the Navy and, from there, back home to live with Ma." The kitten helped, and Jim was grateful Carol found her on the porch. He and Penny would no longer be two lonely souls.

Carol was organized and already had the information to make an appointment for the building inspector to activate the B&B application. Everything was moving along nicely. Jim was seeing Randy's secretary, Mamie, next weekend too. Although Rob had a problem with Randy, Jim was grateful for all the help and advice Randy offered. He was better as a big brother than Rob was.

24

GETTING STARTED

Carol received a call from Alex Graham, Westmoreland County building inspector, early Monday morning. He came the next afternoon. "Is this Webster House? Nice place you got here. What is the history of the house?"

Carol told him, "This land was originally pastureland on my great-grandfather Webster's farm. His original log cabin is long gone. His large barn was struck by lightning and burned back in the eighties, taking the chicken coop too. My grandparents, who had seven children, built this farmhouse. The house was added onto several times to become what it is today. When Grandpa Webster's black lung disease made him too ill to work, their oldest son, my father Walter Webster, primarily a coal miner, brought home his bride to help his mother manage the farm.

"That was when the last extension was built onto the house. Altogether, there are eight bedrooms and four bathrooms. When all my aunts and uncles married and moved into their own homes, Dad fixed up a garage apartment for Gran to move into, and she let my family have the whole house. When Rob and I moved out, the house's west end was closed off to save on heating costs. However, Jim and I are going to get all rooms revamped, including in the additions."

"Monumental task, I'm sure. I moved here just three years ago, so I never knew your father. However, I did get to know your mother somewhat through her efforts to upgrade this town. I have driven by and admired this house and surrounding property. You are one lucky lady, Miz Carol, to own such a fine place. Let's see what we can do to get your bed-and-breakfast approved and operating."

Mr. Graham walked around outside and then went inside, going through each room while making notes on a legal pad he carried on his clipboard. Before leaving, Mr. Graham tore off three pages of notes he made and handed them to Carol. Then, he got out a notebook and wrote phone numbers of the Westmoreland County Health Department and a geological inspector to give her. "You need to make sure there aren't any mine shafts or tunnels under your property. No use doing a lot of work to get approved then have everything slide into a big sinkhole. I think you are safe on that issue since the mine was on the other side of town. But no way of knowing which way all those tunnels went. Now, you have a good day, ma'am."

Jim came home from The Company Store that evening to a frustrated Carol. She read aloud from Mr. Graham's long list of things to do before they could even think about opening the house as a B&B. For starters, they needed to install three sinks in the kitchen (one for washing dishes, one for food preparation, one for washing hands), purchase and install a commercial dishwasher, install fire/smoke alarms and extinguishers near each bedroom, install carbon dioxide detectors, replace loose rugs with either installed carpeting or hardwood floors, install safety bars in all public-use bathrooms, bring railings on porches up to code, add handrails on all stairways, have the furnace cleaned and checked, install a water softener, and install privacy locks on each intended rental space.

She stopped reading to catch her breath and look at Jim with an expression of fear and confusion. She handed the list to him and went back to supper preparation. The list went on and on. In addition, the building inspector would "overlook the lack of an automatic sprinkler system if candles were not used in the house except for dining room table and only if someone were present in the room at all times candles were lit."

He read three legal pad pages of items to be completed. "When am I gonna have time to do all this, Carol? I have a store to run too, ya know? You better look around for a handyman. I'll supply materials." Susie and Carol served supper in the kitchen, and they glumly sat and ate.

Carol made a copy of the list for him while Susie cleaned up after supper. He initialed some of the simpler things he would do on weekends or evenings. "You can use inheritance money and find someone to do the remaining items on this list," he said as he patted her on the shoulder before he went up to his room since he had not yet moved to Gran's apartment. He would be lonely out there, and he was enjoying having the house feeling alive again with Susie's chatter. Penny followed him up the stairs and curled up on the chair in his room. She would be on his bed before morning.

25

JONATHAN MICHAEL HARRISON

Jonathan sat at his office desk at Harrison's Construction Company wondering where to begin now that he had rearranged and placed his parents' furniture into his house. People were taking vacations while their children were out of school for the summer, so home improvement projects were on hold for now. He called several clients and lined up projects with mid-September starting dates. He intended to stay with twin brother Jacob longer, but he couldn't pass up an opportunity to spend more time with Carol Murray. He felt he owed her something. He would find some way to help as she established a new life in Pennsylvania.

He certainly wasn't looking for a relationship, feeling he wasn't good at relationships since his brief marriage did not end well. He was grateful for not having any children to leave behind. At forty-two years old, he concentrated on his work. He stared out the window awhile longer, remembering the past, and then shook his head to clear unpleasant visions from his mind.

That was a long time ago. No use looking backward when a person can't change the past. He picked up the phone and punched in a series of numbers without fully realizing what he was doing. When he heard her sweet voice say hello, he stammered, "Ah…hi, Carol? This is Jonathan Harrison. I was wondering…ah…how you are doing. Have you…ah…gotten your building permits for the B&B yet?"

Carol was surprised to hear his voice, "Yes, the building inspector was here yesterday. Permits are posted in the front windows. I have quite a long list of things to do to get this old house ready for operation as a B&B. My brother, Jim, is busy running The Company Store; and I don't know how to do these improvements. I will be looking for a handy man to complete all requirements." Teasingly, she added, "You don't know of anyone who is handy with tools, do you?" She read some of the items on the list to him.

"Just so happens I do know someone. Will I do? Could I come by and see what is involved? I have given my crew this three-week period off for vacation before our busy fall season begins. I could knock out some of those items before September." Jonathan was getting excited about spending time helping Carol.

Carol continued, "To protect the buildings, I still need to have a survey done by a geological expert to be sure there isn't a mine tunnel or shaft under the house to cause a sinkhole and everything we worked for to fall into an abandoned mine. I need to have the water tested for unsafe particulates, and I am not sure what else. I have to get everything ready for three different inspectors. Ma paid for a permit for establishing a bed-and-breakfast. However, she didn't leave any instructions on how to continue to meet code requirements. I am a little overwhelmed at this point."

Jonathan heard her frustration as her voice climbed a notch higher with each sentence. "Don't give up before you have begun. I will come over on Friday to check the list and talk with your brother and find the best way to get this done." He wished he could leave right away to comfort her, but he would load some tools and go to Lucerne after he had a chance to talk to some experts about B&B county requirements.

On Friday morning, he headed to Lucerne and Carol's new home. She greeted him with a smile and a cup of delicious coffee. He saw Susie again, Carol's daughter, and realized she was a knockout like her mother but just a kid. Besides, he was helping out a lady in distress. A good-looking one for sure, but he would ignore that fact. There is work to be done, and he was there to help.

He and Carol went to The Company Store to meet with Jim and go over the inspector's list. Jim welcomed the help and seemed like an okay guy. They talked about their military days, both having been Navy men. Jonathan served on a destroyer, and Jim spent his time as an aircraft mechanic on a carrier. However, they liked each other instantly. "Let's get the job done so you and your sister can get this B&B open, okay?" Jonathan stated, and Jim agreed. With the two guys' heads bent over the list of improvements, deciding who would do which chore and Jim making a list of materials to take home, Carol left to go grocery shopping since Jonathan agreed to stay for supper.

Jonathan came back to the house and spent the afternoon making his own list of what tools would be needed, checking code requirements, and taking measurements. He checked supplies Jim stashed in the back garage to establish a plan of what to do first. After conferring with Carol to get her input, he called in some orders from his contacts in the building industry.

26

CAROL

They were sitting down to supper when dark clouds rolled overhead. Thunder and lightning soon followed. Although Jonathan's place wasn't far, it wasn't safe to travel. Jim spoke up, "We have an apartment above the garage I have cleaned out and prepared to eventually move into. If you would like, you could stay there tonight. This storm could last awhile. As you know, these mountain roads can be dangerous in this weather. I have some clothes you can borrow. Please stay. We can spend more time this evening and tomorrow morning talking about our project since my helper is opening the store in the morning. We might knock out some of these simpler chores. I brought home more needed materials this evening."

Jonathan accepted graciously. "I don't relish getting out in this weather. Pickups don't have a lot of traction unless loaded down. Thanks. I'll take you up on your offer if it is okay with Carol."

Both guys looked at her. "No problem for me. That space is ready for Jim to move out there, but until he does, it's available. I just need to send out fresh sheets and towels. Breakfast will be ready at seven."

Susie and Carol did a quick kitchen cleanup while the guys talked, and the four of them played Scrabble for an hour before heading off to bed. Jim took Jonathan through the garage, up the stairs, and showed him Gran's apartment. Jonathan was pleased with the room and graciously accepted some denims and T-shirts already in the dresser. The bathroom was already equipped with essentials. Jim made the bed and hung towels in the bathroom.

Carol and Jim talked a while longer after Jonathan retired for the night. "What do you think of Jonathan? Are you okay with hiring him to do the work?" Carol asked.

Jim answered, "He seems like a really nice fellow. I know he has to be smart to do what he did in the Navy. He owns his own company now, but there is a strange sadness to him. Once in a while, he looks off into the distance and seems far away. Says he has lived in Williamstown for about fifteen years."

"Everyone has their secrets, I suppose. Not that I am interested in him other than to do the work on our list of requirements," Carol clarified.

"Of course not," Jim said with a glimmer in his eyes. "That couldn't ever happen." He went up to his room, and Carol lingered awhile, wishing she could have talked to Jonathan a little longer. He seemed lonely. She wasn't looking for a relationship, but having a friend her own age would be nice. She picked up the list of B&B requirements to be completed and noted how many items were initialed JH. Jonathan Harrison would be around quite a bit. She went to her room with happy thoughts of having him around during renovations. In fact, she spent a long time getting to sleep knowing how close by he was. She hoped he was comfortable.

27

RANDY

Randy stopped by the Webster's house a week later and found a strange man adding balusters and new railings to the front porch. He heard via the grapevine there was a stranger in town. Jim mentioned a hired handyman when Randy stopped by the store to ask how preparations were going, but he didn't expect this healthy specimen of masculinity.

Randy felt this tall handyman was a bit too good-looking: a sweat-soaked T-shirt, tight jeans, ball cap perched on the back of his head to shade his piercing blue eyes, and an abundance of brown curls peeking out from underneath his ball cap. Randy was aware of his own stocky build and thinning graying hair. He did run as often as possible, trying to stay in shape. He reached out a hand. "Hello. I'm Randy Block, here to check on Carol and Jim. Are either of them here?"

Jonathan responded as he reached out with a friendly but strong handshake. "I'm Jonathan Harrison, here to help get the house ready for B&B inspections. I think Carol is in the kitchen with Susie making some lemonade, and Jim hasn't come back from work yet. Have a seat," he said, indicating the porch swing with his left hand.

"I didn't know she needed help. How kind of you to help out. Are you from around here?" Randy asked as he made himself comfortable on the swing.

Jonathan looked up from the railing he was installing and wiped sweat from his eyes with a handkerchief, which he stuffed back into his back pocket. Timing his words between hammer swings, he replied, "I helped Carol with her Camry when she had a car problem. My brother did the repair. Just a coincidence my brother and I were behind her when her car acted up. We have sort of become friends since then. I helped her move since I actually live in Williamstown and wanted to help them get their business going. My company is taking a bit of a breather right now. Thought I would keep myself busy for a good cause."

Carol came out the screen door carrying a tray with two glasses of freshly made lemonade. Randy felt overdressed since he was wearing a suit, not tight jeans and a T-shirt, which must be the uniform for today. "Thought I heard voices out here. Thanks for stopping by, Randy. I'll get another glassful of lemonade." She disappeared for a minute and hurried back outside. "I see you have met Jonathan. He is making short work of a long list Alex Graham gave us to complete before the next inspection. I hope to be open for leaf season this fall. Jim and I, and especially Jonathan, have put in a good number of hours toward our goal. It's quitting time. Susie will have meatloaf, mashed potatoes, and broccoli ready in about fifteen minutes. I could set another place if you would like to stay? The more the merrier."

Randy hesitated and then added, "Sure, you can fill me in on what still needs doing. I didn't know you needed to hire help. I can spend part of my weekend helping out. I am fairly proficient with a hammer too, enjoying manual labor to get away from my desk. You know I would do anything to help."

Carol was taken aback by Randy's attitude. Was he jealous? He certainly had no right to be. He was helping in other ways, getting a land survey set up for Wednesday and arranging for Mr. Graham's inspections. She certainly did not feel she led him on by having a business lunch last week.

Supper went well with Susie's chatter about going to college soon and the guys discussing Penn State football after they made a list of what they would work on tomorrow, adding Randy's initials to some items for the upcoming weekend. Carol sat back and observed these three men in her life, doing a mental comparison.

Randy seemed to be playing a game of one-upmanship. She was happy Jonathan and Jim got along and worked well together. Jonathan excused himself and said he would be back early in the morning. He picked up Penny for a minute on his way out to his truck and scratched her neck to set her purring before setting her back down gently onto the back porch swing.

28

INSPECTIONS

Wednesday was another important day. A burly man got out of his car and rang the doorbell asking, "Is this Webster House?" as he removed his hat when Carol opened the door.

Carol said, "We haven't decided on a name for our B&B yet, but Webster House sounds good. My name is Carol Murray, but I used to be a Webster. How may I help you?"

The inspector introduced himself, "I'm Earl Bouch, the geological inspector. I need to take all kinds of measurements: distance from road to house, to back garage, to markers where you want to put a horse stable, to location of well serving the house." After doing all the measuring, he got back in his car, adding, "I need to compare these numbers with the geological survey at the courthouse. I should finish my report in three days."

As he was leaving the driveway, another vehicle pulled in. The plump-faced, red-haired, well-dressed young lady got out of her car with a seal on the door that read Westmoreland County Health Department. Carol shook hands, "I am Carol Murray, part owner of the house. May I help you?"

"Hello. Is this Webster House? If it is, I am Sandy Reynolds from Westmorland County Health Department." She handed Carol her card, and pointed to an ID badge on her lapel. "I am here to do a potable water test as well as check on your plans for food and linen storage, just a general pre-inspection," she replied.

Carol said, "We are far from open for business, and we haven't settled on a name yet. But everyone is calling it Webster House. We might start with that."

Ms. Reynolds responded, "Yes, we are aware of the developing status. However, if there is a problem with the well water test, you will have time to make corrections. There will be several inspections before a final inspection prior to opening. You may as well know what we want so you don't have to redo to meet requirements," she mentioned while handing Carol some paperwork to fill out and proceeding into the house. "In addition, we have the right to make surprise inspections any time we want after you are operating. We will check water, storage of linens, food storage and preparation area in kitchen, dining room, and food equipment cleanliness. We will check for proper operation of fire and smoke detectors, fire extinguishers, and cleanliness of guest rooms, provided they aren't occupied. We never disturb your guests."

Carol barely had time to say, "Pleased to meet you," before Ms. Reynolds continued. "I think you went to school with my mother, Mary Lou Johnston, now Reynolds. Welcome back to Lucerne. This town needs an establishment like yours. The newer hotels are too fancy. We need a place to represent what is unique about Lucerne—the friendly, family-style settings. Don't get nervous. I am here to help you, not to give you a hard time. Relax and let's check out what you need to do to get started." She was smiling, yet her efficiency and forthright attitude was intimidating to Carol.

Carol showed her everything she asked for but did not relax during the inspection tour of the house. She wasn't ready for this. Susie's boxes were stacked up in her bedroom, and the restaurant-style coffee maker wasn't even ordered yet. She explained all this to Ms. Reynolds and was dismissed with a wave of her dainty hand with green-painted fingernails. When Jonathan walked through to install handrails in the upstairs bathrooms, they passed in the hallway. Ms. Reynolds made a comment, "Well, I see your carpenter would pass my inspection any time." She snickered and went on with her walkthrough.

With the health inspection tour completed, Carol walked Ms. Reynolds to her car and was given two more sheets of paper with items to do before the B&B would be ready to open. She was glad Ma converted to a gas furnace in the basement instead of that old coal monster from her childhood. She would never have been able to keep coal dust under control enough to pass such thorough inspections.

What was she getting into? She felt like running back to Vienna and her simple life she led there—until she saw Jonathan coming down the stairs to get his lunch from his truck. Maybe she belonged here after all. She could get used to having him around. Maybe, when she wasn't his employer…

No, she wouldn't entertain that thought just yet. She wasn't trying to make her life any more complicated than it already was.

She read through the newest list of requirements and started to organize the upstairs closet to meet county specifications, then shared the list with Jonathan when he finished his lunch. They talked about adding a closet in the downstairs pantry and adding more shelves in the laundry room. He needed to add a lock to the upstairs linen closet to keep guests from having access to clean bedding and supplies. They would talk to Jim when he got home about possibly closing in the back porch to expand the kitchen. This whole project was getting more and more complicated.

Removing loose rugs revealed original hardwood floors only needing a light sanding and refinishing. The guys were making good progress on mechanical changes and construction projects, so Carol was redecorating as soon as each room was brought up to code. She always enjoyed decorating, although previously her funds were short. With inheritance funds finally available, she stripped wallpaper; painted walls that Jim had not, taking personal family items out of rooms and closets; and purchased new bedspreads and drapes, stacking them in her room until individual rooms were ready for final touches. Carpet was ordered and installed in rooms where the floors were too damaged to refinish.

The family members long ago removed original dressers as they moved out. Replacement dressers were found in an antique shop in another town, and she enjoyed sanding and giving them a fresh coat of varnish to bring out the wood grain. Some original brass headboards were gleaming brightly from the application of Brasso and elbow grease. One thing for sure, she didn't have any trouble sleeping at night.

She joined the local chamber of commerce; and some hotel or motel owners gave her some hotel supply catalogs where she found good prices on sheets, towels, individual soaps, tissue dispensers, bath mats, and all the little details that make a room comfortable and cozy.

Jonathan was in and out of the house often enough if she needed assistance with moving furniture or had a question about the proper varnish or needed extra towel bars installed. They worked well together and had moments where she wondered if she or he were the one in charge. Then, he would say, "Yes, ma'am," in a way that she knew he respected her position on this project. He stayed over in the garage apartment two or three nights a week to save on commuting time. She was enjoying having him as an extra person at mealtime. She enjoyed his company on those evenings when Jim was attending town council meetings or Susie went to church meetings.

On the last day of August, she walked through the house with her list of items to be completed and realized the day was near when Mr. Graham's list would be totally complete. Then what? Would Jonathan disappear from her life? That night, she didn't sleep well. In spite of fatigue from the day's work, she felt anxious about her future.

Would the B&B be all her mother wanted? Would she ever see Jonathan again? She did everything Mr. Graham wanted. Were there other details she was overlooking? She got up and made a list of questions to ask one of her newest friends at the chamber. Her banking accounts were all set up, credit card contracts were signed, registration forms were sitting ready on her desk, insurance policies were in force.

There was so much to learn about running a business. Up until now, she was always an employee, never the one in charge. For now, she felt she would be able to manage without help, but the day might come…

And somewhere around there, sleep overtook her and she had a few hours of rest before the sun rose over the eastern hills and another day of preparation loomed before her.

29

JONATHAN'S DEPARTURE

A week after Labor Day, Carol drove Susie to Pennsylvania State University to begin her first year of college. On her way back to Lucerne, she realized she was speeding, trying to get home before Jonathan left for the day. That's when she realized how much she looked forward to seeing him each day. She had grown entirely too used to having him around.

She found Jonathan in the kitchen finishing the installation of a third sink. A commercial dishwasher had arrived the previous day and was midway through a test run. An unusually hot spell for September was making the day difficult. Jonathan looked exhausted. She quickly fixed a pitcher of fresh lemonade. Carol said, "Take a break. You are working too hard."

Jonathan gratefully accepted the tall cold glass and leaned against the counter. "My September jobs are starting next week. I need to go home and get materials lined up, but I have enjoyed my time here so much. You and Jim have welcomed me as family. I am sad to leave."

Carol patted his shoulder. "You don't have to stay away, ya know? You aren't so far away. We want you to be part of our adventure here. We couldn't have accomplished Mr. Graham's list of required improvements if you hadn't come into our lives. Jim considers you a friend, and so do I. Please say you will stay in touch. Come by on weekends or when you get a break from your construction jobs. You haven't mentioned any family other than your brother, Jacob, and he isn't close by. Please consider us your family. I wouldn't have it any other way."

Jonathan looked at her a long time before he blurted out, "No, Jacob and I are the only ones left in our family except for two aunts who are still living. I used to have a wife. But that ended badly. I am embarrassed to mention my life before moving to Williamstown. I wanted to get away from her and a messy situation I got myself into. If I am going to be part of your life in the future—and I want to—you need to know who I am."

Carol was shocked. She thought she already knew Jonathan. Since he would be leaving her employ, she felt free to say, "I feel I do know you. You are a hardworking, responsible, and good-looking guy. I am happy to have you in my life." She hesitated and then added quickly, "As a friend." She turned away to hide a warm blush on her cheeks. She knew if their friendship were to grow, they could find happiness together. Carol was trying her best to keep everything professional. "Everyone has a past, Jonathan. My past is nothing to brag about either. Can't we look to the future? Finishing this project is a new beginning for me. Does the past mean so much we have to drag it into today to affect our tomorrows?" She was looking out the window but saw his reflection as he reached for her.

Jonathan reached for her hand, and she turned toward him. He looked so pensive as he lowered his head and spoke softly. "The first time I heard your name, I knew who you were. I also knew I had to do everything I could to help you. You see, I used to live near Holidaysburg, Pennsylvania. I was married to a woman your husband was seeing. I am the one who fired a warning shot, causing his fall that killed him!"

He waited a moment before continuing after seeing shock register on her lovely face. "Please, let me explain. I got home early from a hunting trip. Honestly, I thought he was an intruder climbing up to the second floor. I thought I was protecting my wife who I believed to be alone in our bedroom upstairs since the downstairs was dark, with just a dim light in the bedroom window. She explained later. They heard my truck pull into the driveway, and your husband tried to escape by climbing out onto the porch roof and down the lattice on the side. I had my shotgun in my hand. I shouted for him to stop. He didn't. I fired a warning shot toward the hill behind the house. Some buckshot hit a tree, ricocheted, and hit him. He lost his footing, causing him to fall onto a concrete patio. I am so, so sorry. I caused his death. I have not touched a gun since that night. I swear to you, Carol; the shooting was accidental. The judge thought so, too. I did not go to jail, but I have paid a high price for my part in his death. My wife divorced me after I left my home and my job. I ask God for forgiveness every day. But I can't forgive myself. I am trying to make amends."

Carol stood there, stunned, unable to speak. She was only aware of her hand in Jonathan's. She looked at his hand. *This is the hand that took my husband from me.* She jerked her hand free and looked him in the eye without saying a word. She turned away, walked swiftly out to the back porch, let the door slam behind her, picked up Penny, and sat down on the swing, burying her face in the softness of Penny's fur.

Jonathan started to follow her but thought he should leave her alone. "Goodbye, Carol. I hope you can forgive me someday," he declared through the screen, lingering for a moment while hoping for a response. She said nothing and didn't acknowledge his request. He turned and walked out the front door and out of her life.

When she heard his truck leaving, she released her pent-up tears and let go of her hopes for a new relationship. She would mail him a final check for the work he had accomplished and lock down her personal feelings once more. She would throw herself into building this business. She sealed off the crack Jonathan had created in the protective wall she built around herself after Ted died. She made a vow to not let anyone break through her reinforced shell.

30

RANDY

Randy saw Jonathan's truck leaving town in the middle of the day, driving a little faster than usual. Although he was happy to see him go, he had a strange feeling; something wasn't right. He called Carol. Not getting an answer, he drove over to her house and saw her car was there. He knocked; and she came to the door with red eyes, clutching a sodden handkerchief, holding Penny so tight he was afraid she might be hurting the kitten. One look in her eyes told him she needed a friend.

He put his arms out, and she went to him. He enveloped her in his hug, and she sobbed and sobbed on his shoulder. He held her and told her, "No matter what happened, you are going to be okay. God doesn't give you more than you can handle."

It only made her cry harder.

A few minutes later, she pulled back and said, "He did it, Randy. Jonathan…" She cried harder while Randy comforted her. Finally able to speak, she broke the news to Randy. "Jonathan is the one who caused Ted's death. He told me the whole story. I never gave much thought to the other people involved. At the time, I was angry, hurt, confused, and focused on raising my children. I barely took time to grieve. I buried my husband and went on. We didn't have much of a marriage, I admit. With the passing of time, I knew I never really loved him. I married him to get away from Lucerne. However, he did give me my two daughters. Now I am back in Lucerne, making a new life for my daughters and myself back with my family and friends, back in this old house. I am grieving losing so much of my life, and for Jonathan's losses. Sorry. I am a mess. I appreciate your shoulder to cry on and your friendship. How can I repay your kindness?"

Randy gently led her over to the couch where they sat down. He held her hand while saying, "Carol, I never really stopped loving you. You may have left Lucerne, but you never left my heart. I helped your mother in order to stay close to you, to help Jim, to make it up to Rob for stealing his scholarship. A lot of water has gone under the bridge, but God's angels have brought you back into my life."

For the second time today, she looked at the hand holding hers. This one felt right. She didn't pull away. "I think, in time, I can forgive myself for all the things I have done to contribute to the errors of my life. If you can give me a little more time, I will consider starting over with you. I always felt a deep affection for you. You know that, Randy. Right now, I need time to process all I learned today. I need to get the B&B open before I can make promises. I hope you understand."

Randy smiled and dried her tear-streaked face. "Of course I understand. Life has a way of teaching us lessons. Some are tough to swallow. I married for all the wrong reasons too. When you are young, you don't see the big picture. All I know is I am happy to have you back in town, back in my life. I am content, for now, to be your friend as long as you promise me you will think about a future we could have together. Give me a chance to show you how much I care for you. Have lunch with me occasionally. I am willing to wait, but my patience is not unlimited."

Still holding the kitten, Carol agreed to think about Randy in a new light. She invited him to stay for supper and went to the kitchen to check the crockpot she started earlier to share this evening with Jonathan. She looked at the new sink. Jonathan had finished the list. She accepted she might never see him again.

31

CAROL

Time was moving swiftly by. Jim did a few more touch-ups over the next few weeks, and Carol put finishing touches on the decor in each room. Photographs of the farm in its early days were framed and hung on walls. Carol called Mr. Graham on a Friday to tell him the list of requirements was completed.

Mr. Graham said, "I'll be out someday next week for final inspection and issuance of the occupancy permit *if* all is in order. See you then."

She fussed and fussed all weekend, checking and rechecking all details, plumping up pillows, sweeping cobwebs from corners, counting supplies. She and Jim made advertising posters to hang in local stores, wrote advertisements for various newspapers within a fifty-mile radius, and created a brochure to mail out to people who phoned for reservations.

Mr. Graham arrived Monday morning at eight thirty when she was finishing their breakfast dishes. She answered the door while still drying her hands with a dishtowel. Mr. Graham walked around outside inspecting the buildings. Then, he went inside to inspect the basement first, then explored the main floor and climbed the stairs and looked over all the rooms, checking for smoke/fire alarms, carbon dioxide detectors, safety bars in bathrooms, window screens, locks, and everything else on his list to be sure her customers would be safe.

Several times, he made notes in his notebook, which worried her. His inspection was complete. In addition to an occupancy permit, he reviewed the geological results Carol had in her file—no complications from underground mines as far as the house and garage. One recommendation was to relocate the future horse stable for cautionary reasons; an underground mine was within 500 feet, with a margin of error making the location risky. However, the stable was also put on hold. "We plan to revisit that idea next summer," she said.

Mr. Graham left the driveway just as Ms. Reynolds from the Health Department arrived. Carol walked through all the rooms again with her, checking the laundry, linen storage areas, food storage, both refrigerators, and a freezer holding ice for guests' use. Carol plumped a few pillows here and there out of nervousness. Ms. Reynolds asked, "Where is your carpenter today?"

"He doesn't work here anymore. I doubt I will ever see him again."

"Oh…too bad. I suspect he would be good to have around." She sounded disappointed. "Here is your health certificate. We aren't allowed to give one hundreds. But you came close. You need to post this where your arriving guests can see it. Most people frame this and your occupancy permit from Mr. Graham. Remember, I might pop in on you without notice, just as I did today. But don't worry. I don't bite."

Carol looked at the paper she was handed and saw the score of ninety-nine in big red numbers. "Thank you, Ms. Reynolds. I'm glad we meet with your approval. This has been a lot of hard work." She walked with her to the door.

"Oh, don't thank me. You earned it. See you next time." With a little wink, Ms. Reynolds waved and was gone, and Webster House B&B was official.

Carol closed the door and did a little happy dance, and then realized she still had her dishtowel where she had flung it over her shoulder. She called Jim. "Jim, we are officially inspected and licensed. Do you have two document frames you could bring home from the store? I need to frame these official documents for display. Thanks to you and Jonathan, we have something to celebrate."

With some time to spare, since everything was finally ready, she and Jim spent some time doing some outside decor. They created a memorial garden to honor their dearly departed loved ones. They got some river rocks, painted them, then added special names, like Emma, Walter, Aunt Ethel, Uncles Robert and Ronald, and on through the list of those who had gone before. These rocks were placed as decorations throughout a new flower garden. Some climbing blaze roses were planted on each side of a new arbor in the backyard, the romantic setting for any outdoor weddings to be held at Webster House.

With that last planned detail completed, Carol and Webster House were ready for October 2, their opening day, when two local teachers booked Webster House for their wedding under the new rose arbor in the back lawn, and some out-of-town guests were staying for two nights. She hoped all would go well. She couldn't conceive of ever getting married again, yet she was happy others still believed in the sanctity of marriage. She wanted to help this young couple make their day extra special.

Since the following day would be her fortieth birthday, Rob and her daughters would be there to help out while also celebrating a significant birthday. Family was going to take up two of her available rooms. Perhaps she could talk Rob into sharing the garage apartment since Jim was going to stay there for at least the weekend.

She also broke with male-being-the-caller tradition and called Jonathan. "I accept your story of Ted's accidental death. I am sincerely trying to forgive you since you held no malice. You were only protecting your wife and property. Ted was a scoundrel and womanizer, and there were probably many others who would have harmed him if you hadn't. As I said earlier, no use dragging yesterday around and ruining today."

Jonathan was happy to hear from her. "Sure, Carol. I would love to see you and be part of the official opening of your B&B. I'm sure you and Jim have made more improvements since the day I left the job. Oh, and thanks for that final check."

Before opening day, there were a few legal details to complete. Randy drew up papers to divide Ma's holdings. The town properties were to be held in Jaroc's name, with Jim and Carol as coadministrators. As far as Webster House was concerned, Carol received 55 percent, Jim was granted 35 percent, and Rob got 10 percent. Rob wanted to be included as a silent partner, yet both brothers realized Carol would be boss. Jim had the store 100 percent. The balance of Rob's inheritance was in cash, which he wanted in investments for now. He would keep an open mind about how, or if, he would become more involved in the future of Lucerne. Airline pilots can be medically out of a job too easily. He would keep his options open.

"Randy," Carol added when they were ready to leave his office after signing all the official papers, "could you tell me one more thing? How do I go about changing my name back to Webster?"

The guys all turned and looked at her, first with surprise then with big grins. "You really want to do that?" asked Rob and Randy at the same time.

"Yes. If we are calling it Webster House, then I want to be Carol Webster, lady of the manor." She had a sly grin on her pretty face.

Randy struggled to keep his voice professional. "You will have to go to the courthouse in Greensburg, fill out some forms, then go before a judge. I know the judges there and will explain the situation to them. Changing your name should be a simple matter. I'll try to rush the proceedings through for you." He was secretly hoping Carol would be taking his name in the future, but he remembered his promise to not pressure her.

Just ten days later, Carol Murray made the trip to Greensburg to proudly stand before Judge Weinhoff of Westmoreland County to declare, "I want to take back my maiden name, not for any illegal reasons, hiding from debtors, or for the purpose of defrauding anyone but because I am proud of my Pennsylvania heritage and proud to be a part of the reconstruction efforts of my hometown of Lucerne. I do not want to continue to carry my deceased husband's name as a reminder of a man who did not honor our vows."

"Ma'am, I have read your petition to this court, and I agree with you wholeheartedly. You will, from this moment in time, be once more Carol Jean Webster so you may honor your parents and continue being an upstanding citizen of Westmoreland County. Petition granted! Congratulations, Ms. Webster," he confirmed as he tapped his gavel, then reached out and shook her hand.

32

OPENING WEEKEND

As guests and family were arriving on Friday evening for the wedding weekend, Carol was enjoying the attention of everyone admiring the B&B and the results of her decorating skills. Everything was going well. Randy came by with a potted plant for the foyer and openly gave her a hug and a kiss on her cheek. Rob and Jim were going to tease her about that later.

There was a temporary lull in conversation and some strange looks when Jonathan arrived and also gave Carol a hug and a kiss on her cheek. There were no secrets in this small town. She tried to calm her own shaky emotions and introduced Jonathan as the contractor who helped prepare Webster House. The buzz of conversation resumed. She remained aware of him as Jonathan circulated, shaking hands with a number of people.

To some, he handed business cards and made notes in his ever-present notepad. When he approached Randy, he offered his hand, and she saw Randy hesitate. Jonathan said something to Randy that Carol couldn't hear. Randy reluctantly shook hands, then quickly turned away and got a drink from the punch bowl. There was not going to be any friendship there.

When the caterer announced the rehearsal dinner buffet was ready, Pastor Kennedy was asked if he would offer a blessing. Carol used the break in action to calm down and mutter, "Lord, help me in the future."

As everyone was filling their plates, both Jonathan and Randy hovered near Carol. As she went to the long table to sit down, both stood ready to help her. What was she to do?

Just then, the power went off. Jonathan went to the basement to check the power box since he was familiar with the location and had a mini flashlight in his pocket. Carol was told by the Health Department she shouldn't use candles due to the age of the house, but she scampered around and found a few anyway. People were sitting down to eat, and they continued with the limited light of dusk from sparkling clean windows and a few candles on the table. There was an air of celebration, and no one seemed to mind dim lighting. The tension between Randy and Jonathan was eased when Randy realized Jonathan, as a former employee, was familiar with the house and its internal operation.

Tony, the local constable and part of the wedding party, arrived late, saying there was a squirrel in a transformer and the power would be restored momentarily. Carol was relieved when the power came back. Jonathan came up from the basement but stood in the kitchen, ready to go back down if he were needed. The buffet was a huge success; and guests milled about socializing with each other as Carol, Jim, and Rob were swept into a celebratory mood.

Carol kept an eye on Randy and Jonathan, but they seemed to have struck up a friendly conversation at last. She couldn't spend too much time worrying about them. Tomorrow would be another momentous day. These guests were here to attend a wedding to be held under the back yard arbor, and she had too many details to worry about. Two men acting like teenagers were not going to keep her from her appointed tasks.

The next day, it seemed as though the whole town turned out to witness the wedding of two local teachers. They ran out of chairs. People stood along the side of the chairs and on the porch. Carol spread blankets on the ground for people to sit down. As she watched the young bride walk down their new stone pathway to the arbor, she recalled her own courthouse wedding so long ago. How nice it would be to be surrounded by friends and loved ones, being treated as a princess for a day. She allowed herself to be mentally carried away with music, flowers, and feelings of love in the air. She turned to Rob with tears in her eyes as they stood together at the back of the seating area. "Why has this happiness eluded us?" she asked.

Rob put his arm around her as she dabbed her eyes to avoid smudging her makeup. "You still have time, Carol. Don't let happiness slip through your fingers. You are still young with opportunities you don't recognize. Don't let bitterness blind you. Open your heart and your eyes." He nodded toward Randy. "Maybe it's time for you to let go of the past. I still have a problem with Randy, but that's just me. You need to do what you need to do to be happy."

Carol felt a release of pent-up fear and regret as Mendelssohn's familiar composition filled the autumn air in her own backyard. "The old saying is life begins at forty. I am going to turn over a new chapter in my life today and begin anew," she said to Rob as she left his side to sit down next to Randy.

33

WEDDING BELLS

With Carol and Jim sitting on either side of Randy, most wedding guests sat comfortably on new padded chairs for Webster House B&B's first booking. Jim glanced around the green lawn, admiring roses adorning the arbor against a backdrop of green hills and mowed fields where he imagined horses would graze the following summer. The couple standing under the rose arbor was young, smiling, and gazing at each other with total adoration. Jim leaned over Randy to say to Carol, "Someday, I want to feel what they are feeling."

Carol was surprised and nodded in agreement while saying, "Shh," to Jim. She had to admit having the same thoughts. She felt comfortable sitting next to Randy, like wearing old shoes, unlike these dress shoes pinching her toes so used to sneakers. Randy looked at her with a sweet smile and gave her a discreet thumbs-up. She nudged him with her shoulder, happily knowing he was feeling the same thoughts Jim expressed.

Looking around to motion to Rob to come join them, she saw how dejected he looked, and he didn't meet her eye. Instead, he turned and walked slowly off the lawn, up the back steps, and went into the kitchen. She could only imagine what was going on in his mind. He was probably uncomfortable seeing two people so much in love. She wondered if he believed in monogamous relationships. The more the merrier seemed to be his motto when it came to women.

Rob grabbed a beer from the refrigerator and went back to watch the ceremony through the screen door where he could hide his sadness. He said to himself, *Someday, I'll find a mate who has all the qualities I am looking for. Today's women I see aren't like Ma or Carol—women who care about their men, their home, wants children, or wants to settle down. Sure, women are fun at a party, but I want to find a homebody who really cares about me, not how much money I spend on her to show her a good time. Here tonight, gone tomorrow.*

Wistfully, he watched the new Mr. and Mrs. seal their vows with a lingering kiss. He raised his Rolling Rock bottle high in the air for a personal and silent toast, pasted on a smile, and went back outside to join in the celebration. Who doesn't like good food and wedding cake?

During the reception, Jim walked through the crowd carrying a tray filled with glasses of lemonade until it was time to serve the traditional champagne toast. He talked to several of the young ladies who were attendants. Carol saw him pass the tray of drinks to the father of the bride, who took the job without complaining. Jim took the hand of one of the bridesmaids and deftly maneuvered around the temporary dance floor installed on the lawn.

He took a notebook out of his pocket and wrote down a phone number before dancing with another bridesmaid. When all the guests were saying their farewells to the newly married couple, Jim threw birdseed as enthusiastically as everyone. He sidled up to Carol and Rob and grinned with a new verve for life.

34

STRANGERS IN THE MIDST

As wedding guests were leaving Saturday evening, one woman lingered. Carol saw her arrive with a group from town and then, strangely, stayed off by herself, acting as though she didn't really belong. Carol noticed her throughout the afternoon as she wandered in and out of the house several times, although with so many people there, it was hard for Carol to keep track of everyone.

The woman cleared her throat several times as if to speak to Carol, then said nothing. Since Carol was busy saying goodbyes, wishing departing guests safe travel, and receiving many more accolades, this particular woman went outside and sat down on the porch swing. When everyone else was gone, Carol went about her business of setting up for early-morning breakfast, staying close and keeping an eye on the lingering wedding guest, wondering if she wanted to spend the night.

Jim and her daughters pitched in and started changing towels in occupied rooms and stripped the bed in one room where guests had to leave suddenly. They should have it ready soon in case the woman wanted to stay. They followed instructions to not mix wet towels with sheets. They put bins of soiled linens in the laundry room for Carol to do later.

Carol went out onto the porch and sat down on a rocking chair opposite the swing to rest her weary feet. Carol asked, "Is there something I can do for you?"

"No, not right now. I want to introduce myself, however. I am Lisa Weleski Jeffries, just enjoying the peacefulness and wishing your father had not kept so many secrets. He should have let everyone know I existed," she said with a look of contempt. "This property, this B&B, should be partly mine."

Carol was flabbergasted. "Why do you say that? This was my great-grandfather's home before it was my family's home. Why do you think you deserve to have a share?"

"For your information, we have the same father, Miz Carol. Walter Webster had an affair with my mother when she was a sitter for you and your brothers. *Our* father had to deal with all those lonely nights while your mother worked. I am living proof."

"You have to be kidding. My mother would have known," Carol added in disbelief.

"Probably not. She thought her faithful husband was at home watching over the children. There were nights he hired my mother then left to hang out at the bar with the guys. He would come home drunk and sweet-talk my mother into bed with him. Oh, you think you are so much better than those of us who stayed in Lucerne. You don't know the half of it, sister. And I mean that literally." Mrs. Jeffries rose, smoothed her skirt, and walked toward the door. "I will be leaving in a few minutes. Now that I have seen the lovely grounds and home, I have some thinking to do. You will be hearing from me," she said with a toss of her bleached hair, defiantly sticking her nose in the air.

Carol rose quickly from the rocking chair to block Lisa Jeffries' entry into the house. "You might do some extra thinking about what happens when a person attacks my family. I am usually an easygoing person. However, you accused my father, one of the sweetest men who ever lived, of being unfaithful and a drunk, turning his back on you as a child and lying to my mother and all of us. You may have awakened a hibernating bear with your accusations. You will certainly be hearing from me. I want you off my family's property. *Now*." They glared at each other until Lisa broke the stare and slowly turned and went down the steps, walking toward town.

For all her bravery while confronting Lisa Weleski Jeffries, Carol still worried. After all the hard work and expense of getting the B&B licensed and running, could they lose it to this woman who came out of nowhere? Would she, could she, cause real trouble? After she watched this Lisa leave the property, Carol walked back inside and called Rob and Jim to join her on the back porch where she blurted out, "Guys, we may have a problem." She repeated to them what Lisa Jeffries implied.

Rob was furious. "That's not true about Dad, Carol. He was as devoted a husband and father as I could imagine. He loved Ma and us. I don't recall any time he hired a sitter while Ma was at work. He read to us and played games. He taught us how to cast our fishing lines, and he made popcorn. I never knew of him to have more than one beer. He wouldn't do such a thing as this Lisa claimed. I know he wouldn't. I am not married because I haven't found a woman like Ma so I could be as faithful as Dad!"

Jim scratched his chin thoughtfully. "No way, Carol. I agree with Rob. But I think we need to get Randy in on this to protect our interests. I think the only thing we can do is request a DNA sample. If she is for real, we will have to see what she thinks she deserves. If not, we won't spend a lot of time worryin' about nothin'. Let's go see Randy."

"It's too late tonight, Jim. This will have to wait until tomorrow. I'll talk to him in the morning after church." Carol spent a restless night, tossing and turning, wondering how or why Lisa could come up with the basis for such a story. With a firm resolve to get to the bottom of this accusation, she finally fell asleep as the moon illuminated her bedroom only hours before her alarm woke her.

Her waking thoughts were about Lisa Weleski Jeffries. *Weleski? Weleski? Didn't I see something in Ma's notebooks about someone named Weleski? But which notebook? There are too many to remember.* She got out of bed and quickly dressed for the day. When Jim came down for breakfast, she asked him if he recalled reading about someone named Weleski in the notebooks he scanned.

"No, sis. Not that I recall. I don't remember Ma ever mentionin' any problem with anyone by that name or any other for that matter. Like I said, I didn't know any of this was goin' on."

"Thanks, Jim. I'll just hope I can find it again. Maybe Randy remembers."

As soon as breakfast was served and cleaned up, she couldn't wait any longer and called Randy before he left for church. She told him she might have a bit of a problem. "I'll be right over," was all he had to say to calm her nerves.

As he walked in the door, he could see she did not get a good night's sleep. Roberta and Susan stood at the door to say goodbye to the last departing guests while Rob, Jim, and Carol went out to the back porch to brief Randy on the situation.

"Please, don't let this trouble you any longer. The address is 59 De Haven Street, on the corner of Oak, that was rented by a young woman named Lisa Weleski who married Harold Jeffries. The constable had to issue an eviction notice that they kept denying getting. I think…yes, that's their name. They took six months to evacuate and moved over to Waterman. If she is that Lisa Weleski, she has no grounds. All she has is an annoying habit of trying to scam nice people. They left the property in such a mess. It was best to just tear it down. Come to think of it, the fire department burned it for training. That property is the playground behind the library. She is a mean, vindictive person. How do you want me to handle her?"

"I thank you for wanting to help. However, I want to be the one to handle her. I can't rely on others to fight my battles. I have spent most of the night coming up with a plan. I would like a little time to do some research. This is an insult to my family. May I go to church with you today?"

"Sure, I have been wanting you to attend with me. I'd be honored."

After church, Carol talked to the bride's mother who gave Carol some insight. "My daughter went to school with a girl named Lisa, who married a man named Jeffries. She wasn't invited to the wedding but attended anyway. After the Krauses left, they rented their house which was next door to me. When they wanted to sell the house to Jaroc Enterprises, there was some trouble getting them to move out. By the time they did move out, along with all the freeloaders who hung out there, the house was in such poor condition, the fire department burned it for training purposes. She isn't a friend, but I can get their address over in Waterman. My sister lives near them, and they aren't nice neighbors. Good luck with them. I hated to see my neighbors' house burned, but that was the right thing to do. Such a mess! The playground is a welcome addition."

"Thanks for the information, and I do sympathize with you for all the trouble she caused you. I'm getting an idea of who she really is."

Carol went to Ma's office and found the complete story in the De Haven property notebook. While there, the bride's mother called Carol with an address where Lisa Weleski Jeffries could be found.

Carol spent several hours of her next few busy days scanning newspaper articles on microfilm, looking for information on the Jeffries or Weleski families. Several items were found in public notices, including a relative who was a foreman in the BNP Coal Mine Company.

Carol reported to Jim, "I've got her number now. Don't give that woman another thought."

35

RESOLUTION

A week later, Carol didn't waste any time with the woman who opened the door at the address the bride's mother gave her as Randy, Constable Tony, and she stood on the porch outside Lisa's front door. Carol looked around at the shabby condition of the house and a wreck of a car in the driveway. "Hello, Mrs. Jeffries. We need to talk."

"So nice to see you again so soon," Lisa answered in a friendly voice, batting her eyelashes to play up to the attractive men accompanying Carol.

Carol observed the unkempt condition of Lisa's hair and makeup. She didn't look at all like any of her siblings. She looked exactly as Carol suspected she was—someone trying to cause trouble. "I am here to discuss your claim of being my father's illegitimate daughter."

Lisa Jeffries's attitude changed to be on the verge of belligerent as she repeated nearly word for word the same story Carol heard after the wedding, sounding more like a memorized script.

When Lisa finished her lame performance, Carol continued, "There is a simple way to prove your claim. If what you say is true, you won't mind giving us a DNA sample, would you? I have a sterile test kit for you. The constable will witness you swabbing inside both your cheeks then putting the swabs in this sealed tube and resealing it. In this clean plastic bag, surely you wouldn't mind giving us a sample of your hair from a hairbrush?"

"And what if I don't want to?" Lisa asked in a tone of contempt and with an angry toss of her bleached blond hair.

"Well then, we will presume your claim is without merit. Mr. Block is my attorney, and Tony also represents the law. There are laws against causing trouble. Some would call it harassment. Others might call it fraud. Either way, this needs to be resolved by depositions and a thorough investigation to get to the bottom of this accusation." Carol hesitated to let those words and meanings sink into Lisa's mind.

Carol continued when she noticed Lisa begin to squirm, nervously tapping her chipped fingernails on the doorframe and breaking eye contact. "We could go away and pretend this never happened if you are willing to admit you made up this entire flawed story. We would need you to further promise to never bother us again. Which will it be?" she asked as she held out the DNA kit to Lisa.

They were not surprised when Lisa quickly stepped backward and the front door was slammed in their faces. Through thin walls, they heard her yelling, "It didn't work, Harold. I told you these people were too smart to fall for a stupid idea such as that."

Carol and Randy chuckled as they drove back to Lucerne from the nearby town of Waterman. With only two days of research, they already knew about the Jeffries being troublemakers for other townspeople in the past. Ma's notebooks held the information needed. The Jeffries were evicted from one of Ma's homes she purchased. However, they lived there for another six months without paying any rent before they finally moved out, leaving the house in shambles. Harold's father was a foreman at the BNP Coal Company when Emma worked nights. They knew just enough local information to make up this harebrained scam.

Randy reaffirmed, "I don't think you will have any more trouble from that source. Just the same, stay on the alert for other troublemakers. Some people don't take it too well when some people hit it lucky. There are those who want to capitalize on others' good fortunes and hard work. Greed and envy are terrible things. Combine the two, and...well, let's just hope you have smooth sailing from here on out."

Carol told him, "Sorry to take you on this wild goose chase. However, it was a nice day to go for a drive. I could have handled her on my own, but one never knows to what lengths someone will go when confronted. Add your legal time to my bill. I can't thank you enough for looking after me as you do. What would I do without you?"

"I hope you never have to find out. You can pay this bill by having dinner with me on Thursday evening," he simply stated and was thrilled when she agreed.

Tony added his assurance that he would provide more surveillance for them, driving by Webster House more often. The B&B was within his jurisdiction.

36

TRAGEDY

Carol took a drive on a quiet midweek afternoon to visit the graves of her parents since she had not been to the cemetery while so busy getting the B&B up and running. She sat on the lush green grass and told both of them about the many developments in the last few months. There was a lot to tell, and in the long late fall afternoon, shadows reached her and gave her a chill.

As she reached around behind her for her jacket, a fading sunbeam lit a weathered marker she never noticed before with a name barely readable—"Alice Faye Webster, infant daughter of E & W Webster." The dates were unreadable. She would have to look into that to find out if there was something she should know.

Later that evening, she shared this news with Jim. "I visited the cemetery today. I saw a marker with the name Alice Faye Webster. Do you know anything about another child? Did Ma ever mention a baby who died?"

"Not that I recall. But you know she kept a diary as long as I can remember. I think there is a trunk full of them in the attic. Wanna go up and take a look?"

They went up narrow attic stairs, pulled the chain on a bare bulb hanging from the ceiling, and moved aside some dust-covered boxes to pull an old trunk out from between the rafters. The lid creaked open, revealing stacks and stacks of Ma's journals, some dated back to her teenage years.

"I'll go get a box to carry them downstairs so we can get out of this dust." Jim found a box in the garage in the recycle pile and went back up to fill the box with journals covering the early years of their marriage. "I hope Ma doesn't mind our intruding into her privacy."

Carol's curiosity was piqued. Although Ma never spoke of losing a child, she knew there was some kind of sadness in her mother's past. Could this explain it all?

Over the next few evenings, Carol and Jim discovered the truth behind the aversion to Ma entering the library room. Carol read aloud about their parents' joy of discovering the first pregnancy, fixing the room as a nursery, collecting baby furniture from family hand-me-downs or farm sales. Ma described the day she went into early labor and the birth of tiny Alice, who died three days later.

"Sadly, Jim, if Alice Faye had been born in this modern age, she might have lived. We might have had an older sister. However, most preemies back then were too underdeveloped to survive without today's modern medical advances." Heartbreak was evident in their mother's words. She didn't hold anything back while expressing her feelings in the journals covering this tragedy only a year after their marriage.

Her mother's tone changed in the journals when she discovered she was carrying another child. The large house made it possible to select another room for a new nursery. Walter created a library in Alice's nursery for his books he read on those long winter evenings. Rob's current bedroom had been his nursery, and his arrival was celebrated. However, no child could replace the one lost.

37

CHANGING TIMES

In the weeks following the wedding, Jim called and dated each one of his new contacts living within reasonable driving distance. By this time, he was keeping a calendar of who he was seeing and when. He was also making lunch dates with Mamie from Randy's office, doing maintenance around the B&B, and running the store. There were more and more days when he was asking his employees to open in the mornings or close in the evenings. Carol was seeing a new glow in his eyes. She finally stopped worrying about him.

One evening, as they gathered pumpkins from the garden, with the butterfly-chasing Penny trailing along behind, he revealed to her about the planned fire that would have destroyed their home and him along with it. "Jim, I am so happy coffee-ground-dampened papers prevented a fire. What a loss that would have been. And I don't mean the house. You are too precious to lose. Even though I wasn't around much, I never stopped loving you and Ma. You must have a guardian angel."

Jim scuffed his toe in the dirt, afraid to look at Carol for fear she would see tears forming in his eyes. They decorated the porches with pumpkins, and he gave her a hug as they sat down on the porch swing to enjoy a spectacular sunset over the rolling green hills.

Not long after confiding in Carol, Jim decided to keep the store closed on Sundays. One weekend, he asked Carol if it would be all right if he visited an old Navy buddy who lived across the state line in Maryland. Webster House was usually full of paying guests on weekends, and he couldn't do any maintenance or make noise with mowers and such. He must have had a good time with his friend since visiting him became his favorite weekend activity.

Carol spent Tuesdays at Ma's office. She didn't have the heart to change the name on the door. She had the local sign painter add "and C. J. Webster" below her mother's name. Randy usually had court on Tuesdays. If he didn't, they would drive to the nearby Eat'n Park to have lunch. They were enjoying being good friends for the time being. Carol knew he wanted more. She was too busy getting used to her new lifestyle to get any more involved.

She also called Mr. Gardner at the newspaper in Virginia. "I am having too much trouble finding quiet time to sit and write my weekly column. I really need to give up writing for the newspaper. I have built a successful business and need to concentrate on running it."

"Your stories are interesting. I do hope you will submit articles about the B&B when you have time. I do wish you well in your future. Maybe the wife and I will come to visit you sometime."

She and Jim expanded their initial Webster House advertising brochure. Her contacts within the local chamber of commerce and referrals from other business owners in town helped keep the rooms filled to capacity. She met and made friends with more folks in the hospitality industry; some had been friends from her high school days. She was really becoming an integral part of the community once more.

Folks came from many southern states to enjoy a colorful leaf season of the many deciduous trees. Mother Nature painted the landscape yellow, orange, red, and brown before the trees shed their leaves, which turned rolling hills brown with bare trees forming fringed ridges. The ski slopes would be opening soon, triggering plans to prepare for winter guests.

This would be a colder year for Carol. She would miss the slightly warmer Virginia climate. They were so busy, Carol idly mentioned to Pastor Kennedy's wife after church services in late October she could use some help.

38

A NEWCOMER

Pastor Kennedy, from Lucerne's Fellowship Presbyterian Church, got a call from Constable Tony on October 20 at 7:37 p.m. concerning a young woman who had been in and around the town square most of the afternoon. "She has been sitting on that same park bench since six. During my security rounds of closed businesses, I observed her eating one hard-boiled egg and looks as though she is preparing to sleep there on the bench. It's a mild night but not a good idea to sleep in the park."

"Come on, Rachel. There is a young woman possibly needing some assistance. You'd better go along."

When the pastor and his wife arrived, they found a young woman with only a stuffed duffel bag for a pillow. Her hair had been crudely cut to shoulder-length, and she was quite evasive when questioned about why she was in town. "Who are you visiting? We will take you to them."

She really hesitated before answering "Cousin Katie, but I find she is away."

Pastor Kennedy knew quite a few folks around town, and he didn't recognize the name. Taken as a runaway, although older than most runaways, Pastor and Mrs. Kennedy invited her to the rectory. She reluctantly walked with them the short distance to their small house next to the church while firmly clutching her duffel bag.

They warmed some leftovers from their more than adequate supper while assuring her she would be safe to rest there in their guest room.

While she ate, tears started to flow. Between sobs, she told them a little of her story. "My name is Martha Louise Yoder. I come to town with deliveryman and do not vant to go home. Please, do not tell single soul vhy I am here. I do not vant to shame Papa. He promised me to marry a man I vould not. The man vants to make me his slave. His children are not vell behaved. He is old, fat, and ugly. Please, I vould be forever in your debt." She dried her eyes on a handkerchief she kept tucked up her sleeve.

"We promise to protect you and give you sanctuary. We will keep your secret and not tell anyone of your plight," Mrs. Kennedy assured her. "We will do whatever we can to make you feel welcome in Lucerne and help you find a place where you can create a new life. Recently, we heard of a job opening to suit you. You know how to cook and clean, and there are other places just like Webster House in case Miz Carol doesn't need full-time help."

Martha had a restless night's sleep but felt safe. After breakfast, Mrs. Kennedy said, "Why don't we do some trimming of your hair to give you a softer look?"

Martha agreed and calmly sat in a kitchen chair while Mrs. Kennedy cut her hair and showed her how to fluff it up instead of being pulled back so severely. Together, they shortened one of Martha's dresses to a proper length and gave her a pair of shoes more fitting to her outfit instead of the clodhoppers she wore.

"Let's go look through donations for the monthly church rummage sale for other garments you could use." By the time Mrs. Kennedy was finished, Martha did not look at all like a runaway Amish woman. Her new hairstyle softened her features, showing her to be quite attractive. Mrs. Kennedy said, "I doubt your papa would recognize you if you met him on the sidewalk. Your disguise is your own natural beauty." They worked a little on the way she talked, with Mrs. Kennedy giving Martha proper English words for her Pennsylvania Dutch language. Martha practiced how to walk with her chin up and how to say yes instead of yah.

"Perhaps you would consider making a bit of a name change since Yoder may be recognized. Martha is a common enough name. What was your mother's maiden name?"

"She vas a Smith from Smithport."

"Perfect. Smith is a very common name around here." Thus, Martha Smith arrived in Lucerne. "Since we are all God's children, I will tell Miz Carol you are my cousin needing work. She owns a lot of property around town and will probably have a place for you to stay also."

39

MARTHA SMITH

Mrs. Kennedy showed Martha around town to get her oriented on how to find stores she might need in the future. When she was introduced to Jim, owner of The Company Store, he did not show any sign of recognizing she was briefly in the store the day before.

On October 21, Carol received a call from the pastor's wife. Mrs. Kennedy asked if it would be all right to come by with a cousin of hers needing a job. "Didn't you did tell me recently you were looking for a helper for some part-time work? Well, I think I have someone to fit the bill. If it is okay, we'll come right over."

"Sure, come on by. I could use some help, but not full time. Business has slacked off since the leaves have all dropped. Tourist season is taking a break until ski season starts."

Mrs. Kennedy and Martha Smith arrived twenty minutes later. "Carol, this is my cousin, Martha Smith. She needs a job and a place to live. Do you have any positions open or apartments for rent? Martha, this is Carol Webster, owner of Webster House and a few other properties around town."

Martha said, "So pleased to make your acquaintance, Ms. Webster. I am a goot worker, quiet and clean."

The young woman impressed Carol. There was something serene about her, with an air of inner beauty and natural charm, although she seemed a bit shy. Her hair was cut shoulder-length with bangs and had natural red highlights. Her simple dress and sensible shoes indicated she was ready to work. Carol took them both straight to the kitchen and served some hot coffee.

Martha marveled at all the modern equipment and let her eyes travel around the kitchen, studying a coffee maker, toaster, and a box called a microwave oven, wondering how everything worked. There was a small room off the kitchen with shiny white appliances and shelves stacked with clean sheets and towels.

Carol figured out the young woman was new to town. She heard rumors about all Mrs. Kennedy's 'cousins' she rescued. So Carol went along with the pretense. She caught a wink Mrs. Kennedy gave her while Martha wasn't looking. Living close to the Amish, there were always a few who wanted to get away from the Spartan lifestyle for one reason or another. *Isn't that what I did*, she thought. *Run away from a life I didn't want? Look at me now. Here I am back. No one is better equipped to help Martha than I. I will do what I can.*

"Martha, it would please me if you called me Carol. You can help in the kitchen and do some light maid duties, like making beds, dusting, cleaning upstairs bathrooms—"

"You have bathrooms inside, ma'am? Oh, sorry to interrupt. You will have to show me how to do cleaning in bathrooms. The rest I already know."

Carol hid her smile. Just as she thought, but she didn't mind. "Yes, Martha, I will work with you until you learn the routine. I don't really need full-time help, especially this time of year. However, I have become acquainted with some motel managers and will introduce you to them after you learn what the job here involves. Your last name is Smith? My mother was also a Smith before she married. Perhaps you are my cousin as well." Soon, Carol and Martha were chatting like two old friends.

"Mrs. Kennedy said you might know of a place for me to stay. I am used to simple life, don't need anything fancy. I spent last night with Pastor and Mrs. Kennedy. I will work hard, ma'am, to pay you back."

Carol had no qualms in offering her the garage apartment. Jim didn't seem to be moving out there any time soon. May as well put it to good use for a person in need. Martha looked as though she might cry when Carol said, "You can stay here. We have a small apartment above the garage. For now, we will consider you a guest of the family. Will that be all right?"

"Yah... I mean, yes, ma'am. That would please me very much." Martha clasped her hands together in a prayerful gesture that touched Carol's heart.

Mrs. Kennedy breathed a sigh of relief. It was a good thing she was good at keeping secrets. Sometimes, a preacher's wife got very involved in doing the Lord's work. Mrs. Kennedy excused herself, leaving Martha in good hands with Carol. She quietly placed Martha's duffel bag and a small suitcase inside the front door.

When Jim came home from the store that evening, he was pleased to see Carol had found someone to help around Webster House. "Yes, hello again, Martha. You came into the store earlier with Mrs. Kennedy, right?"

"Yes, so good to see you again," she mumbled as she turned her back and helped set the table and serve supper. She didn't want Jim to see the fear in her eyes or for him to get a good look at her. She kept her head down and didn't talk much during supper. She listened attentively as Jim and Carol told her the history of their house and about growing up there. She didn't need to say much, just nod and say, "Goot night," after dishes were rinsed and put in a box beneath the counter. Carol pushed a button and started all kinds of whooshing sounds.

Martha could not believe her good fortune. Carol took her under her wing and acted nicer than Martha thought her own mother would have if she had not been so sick and died so young. Carol took her through the garage, and Martha saw a fancy car parked in there. She had to bite her tongue to keep from giggling. They went up carpeted stairs, and she was shown a comfortable space above the garage, noting a lot of the same strange items from Mrs. Kennedy's and Carol's kitchen. She didn't want to appear ignorant, so she didn't ask questions.

After Carol showed her how to turn on the television; pointed to the indoor bathroom in the corner; put paper cartons of milk, eggs, and juice in the electric refrigerator; and promised to get it stocked with fresh foods tomorrow, she showed her where to find extra blankets if Martha got cold. Martha was overwhelmed but kept her excitement from showing. She waited until Carol went back downstairs before opening her duffel bag and suitcase full of new-to-her clothes and then placed her few simple items in dresser drawers.

She sat down on a chair by the dressing table to unpack her hairbrush and comb. When she saw her reflection in the mirror, she was shocked. Looking back at her was an attractive young lady. She had a hard time realizing she could look so pretty. Her shorter haircut gave her angular face a becoming softness. A few good nights' sleep and rest from worrying would take the dark circles from under her bright blue eyes. Mrs. Kennedy gave her some pink cream in a tube to brighten her lips, which seemed to have brought out color in her cheeks too. Of course the color in her cheeks could be from excitement.

Martha continued to sit in front of the mirror, something she was not used to doing. As she brushed her hair, she practiced her words Mrs. Kennedy taught her. *Yes* instead of yah, *no* instead of nah or *nein*, *thank you* instead of *danke*. She practiced saying "Martha Smith" over and over. She pushed the button to turn on the television, but the images were too frightening. Best leave that box alone. She wished she could tell her sisters where she was, then decided it could be dangerous to let Papa find her. He might take her back to the farm and an unwanted marriage.

She hung her dresses in the closet. Some she folded and placed in the bottom dresser drawer, hoping she would not need them. She would not go back to her old life. She would make a new life for herself. Plus, she had new clothes to wear. She went into the bathroom to change and let her comfortable flannel nightgown fall softly over her body, smelling homemade soap from back home and allowing herself to relax.

She turned down the bed to find fine percale sheets, not muslin or flannel. The pillow was not hand-plucked goose down but soft and comfortable. In spite of being quite weary, she tossed and turned, reliving the events that brought her to this strange, new place. Although it seemed ancient history, as she did last night, she once more relived the day Papa started it all and the events that followed.

40

MARTHA'S STORY

I couldn't believe what Papa said.

"Mart'a? Did thee hear me?"

"Yah, Papa. I did hear thee. I am considering vat thee say. However, I am tending to disagree with thee, if I may be so bold." I was afraid of vat he might do if I said aloud vat I vas thinking.

"Well, thee vill do what I say, and that is final word on subject," Papa declared, and out he went, slamming the kitchen door as he left. "There are chores to do. I vill not tolerate any back talk or stand around to argue with disobedient daughter," he yelled as he stomped across the porch, down the steps, and headed for the barn.

I was nearly beside myself, partly from fear of Papa, partly from anger and frustration over recent developments. After all I had done to help Mama during her long sickness, and for Papa by running the household and raising younger brother and two sisters after Mama died, I had no say in vat I was allowed to do.

I gave up schooling. I missed all privileges of being young and became old before my time. I missed being courted at proper time. At twenty-four, I did not like being called an old maid by people I knew. My options for marriage were few, mostly to men who lost wives due to sickness or childbirth and already had children needing mothers. That is not vat I vanted for myself.

My limited knowledge of the world beyond the fences of Papa's farm vas restricted to vat I heard while shopping for fabrics at the store in Schmicksburg from visitors who came to services at neighboring farms or stopped at our roadside stand in summer where I sold produce from the garden and my home-baked pies, bread, and sticky buns. I vas not always able to attend services since it seemed one child or another vas sick, causing me to stay home and attend to their sickness.

I remembered a long-ago conversation with a visiting aunt. If I took an entrance exam to become a nurse, I could probably graduate without taking any classes. I have taken care of so many sick people and even delivered babies around the community. While vaiting for babies to arrive, I read books found in their houses to gain schooling I missed.

I remembered all too well the shock of vat I heard Papa say. Papa and I were only ones home, with Horace in school after Labor Day. He say, "I make promise thee vill marry Harvey Brinkerhoff on next Marriage Day Service." Going about my afternoon chores and meal cooking as usual, however, neither Papa nor Horace noticed how quiet I vas or ven I vent to my room after dishes vashed, dried and put away, and breakfast laid out for easy preparation at the crack of dawn.

My goose-down pillow stifled my sobs so Papa vouldn't know of my unhappiness. My prayer to God vas, "Please help me get out of Papa's promise without causing shame to him. I don't vish to hurt him. I only vish to save myself from an unhappy life. Harvey Brinkerhoff is old, fat, and ugly. His three children are the vorst behaved at services. I cannot marry him. I vill not. I vill run away first. I am not needed any more except as cook and housekeeper. Papa is keeping me here until he finds a widow to bring home. I vould not need to stay if I could help him find a mate to take my place."

That was another night I lay awake half the night trying to come up with a plan to escape. I vas vatched so closely, even with youngest brother fifteen and old enough to take care of himself. Sisters are already married. It vas time for me to put a plan into action.

The following Sunday, ven we left services at the McKinnon Farm, I saw a new voman, must have been visitor from another community. I quickly introduced myself to see if she vould fit into my plan. "Hello, I am Martha Yoder. Are thee new to our services? Velcome. I hope thee comes again."

"Ya, I am new here. I am Louisa Heinrick. I come from Ohio to visit my sister who is married to Alvin Hostetler. I von't be here long, just a few weeks to help her in her birthing time."

"Ya, I know thy sister Janette. I plan to be there for her birthing time too. Would thee like to visit my family, and we can get to know each other before we vork together?"

"I vould like that. Danke, Mart'a."

"Come by eleven. Share dinner table with family. Alvin and Janette vill give directions."

Promptly at 10:50, the Hostetler carriage arrived at our hitching post. Louisa deftly dismounted and secured her borrowed horse, gave him some hay, and saw he could reach the watering trough. Papa was just leaving the barn and stood to vatch as she slightly raised her long dress to climb the porch stairs. Her long hair was gathered into an elaborate mass of curls trying to escape her sunbonnet. She hung the bonnet on the family coat hook as she entered the kitchen door.

"Vat could I do to help?" Louisa offered.

"Just fill glasses from brown pitcher and rest of family vill be here in minutes." I barely finished my sentence when Papa and young Horace came in, vent straight to the side sink to vash a bit, and both sat down without a vord of greeting.

"Papa and Horace, this is Louisa, Janette Hostetler's sister, here to help with the birthing of their first child. Remember, I told thee ve vould have guest today?"

"Ya, hello Miz Louisa. Thee and Mart'a will be helpful to young Janette. Let's eat this food the Lord doth provide."

Louisa and I chatted over our dinner plates, and I also noticed Papa listened and vatched with more interest than usual to our conversations. As soon as he cleaned his plate, sopping gravy with his thick slice of bread, he sat down in a soft chair for his regular rest time and Bible reading. Horace vent back outside to finish morning chores, feed chickens, and check vater in horses' trough.

Louisa and I vashed dishes and then sat at the table for some voman talk.

Louisa told me about her short marriage. "Caleb vas ill when ve married. I knew he vould not be living much longer. He had blood disease. Leukemia I think vas called. I think his mama and papa grew tired of caring for him, and my papa promised me to him many years before. I took goot care of him and found happiness in his comfort. We were unable to have children due to his illness. Now I find happiness in caring for others. If it be God's vill, I vill find another mate. If not, I don't need anything more. My in-laws provide for my living as is custom."

"You are lucky to have caring in-laws. Thy sister Janette is lucky to have thee help her in time of need. I have been helping with birthing many years and vill be there ven Janette's time comes if thee still needs my services. Send a message via Alvin ven time comes." We shared some housekeeping hints and a crochet pattern before Louisa said she needed to get back to Janette. Papa got out of his chair, opened the door for Louisa, and made sure her horse's harness was still properly positioned and the horse and carriage backed up from hitching post. I vatched and tried to not show my pleasure.

Papa found several excuses over next few weeks to help Alvin Hostetler with projects around his farm. I vas pleased. The more interest Papa showed in Louisa, the more I envisioned getting away from the farm and promise Papa made for me to marry someone I vould not.

Babies are unpredictable. Instead of only a few weeks, the Hostetler baby did not arrive until the next full moon, almost a month later. By this time, Louisa and Papa had become good friends, taking carriage rides together after Sunday services. Louisa no longer talked about her return to Ohio and vas saying how much Janette could use her help with the baby boy who suffered from colic.

I vas able to focus on my preparation to escape. I made conversations with a truck driver who took Amish quilts and baked goods to stores in nearby towns. I hoped he thought I was just being friendly ven I asked him vere he made stops. The next time I saw him, I asked vat it was like in some of those far-off towns. The next veek, I asked if I could hitch a ride to go see a sick relative in the little town of Lucerne. The town was so small and out of the way, I felt Papa vould not find me there. I vould change my name, cut hair, and get away from farm. Surely, I could find vork somehow with all my skills.

I vaited until Papa and Louisa got closer. One Sunday afternoon, I came in from gathering eggs in the henhouse and found them on porch swing. Papa let go of Louisa's hand but not before I saw. I offered a prayer my attempts at matchmaking had vorked.

After all fall garden produce was stored, I cleaned the house, top to bottom, hiding a duffel bag of my favorite things in the pantry vere Papa never saw. One Tuesday morning, on the day the truck driver normally made his delivery to Lucerne, I dressed with several layers of clothing. I told Papa and Horace at breakfast I vould be away at a birthing and for them to get food from the springhouse for their supper. I took the small duffel out of hiding, added some snacks and a pair of scissors, and valked to town, met the trucker at General Store, and rode out of town into a new life. I didn't know vere I was going; I left the Amish way of life and Schmicksburg behind.

I jostled along in the truck, making happy conversations with truck driver, not letting on vat I was doing. I made a note to send back with the truck driver to be delivered to Papa by the storekeeper after the driver promised to not tell vere he left me. The note read, "I apologize for your shame over the broken promise to Mr. Brinkerhoff. However, I cannot marry a man I do not love, or even like. His children are uncontrollable, and I vould rather live alone in strange city than be wedded to him. I am hitching ride to Philadelphia to find Auntie Grace." I doubted he vould try to find me, especially since Auntie Grace was shunned by the community for marrying out of Amish faith.

Ven truck arrived in Lucerne, I helped carry some lovely quilts into Company Store. The owner, introduced as Jim, made a list of patterns and the quilt maker, and I was helpful with saying pattern names. I looked around at all the fancy gadgets for sale. I watched Mr. Jim ring up a few sales on a machine. Everything vas so strange and new. After saying danke and goodbye to kind driver, I walked around town, in and out of a few stores, ate some bread and ring bologna, and discovered a park bench next to a small lake. I sat and watched the geese and ducks, wondering vhy they didn't leave to go south.

As the afternoon shadows grew long, I vent to a café and had a mug of hot chocolate, careful to not spend too many of the coins I took from the coffee can that morning as I left. I used the indoor ladies room and cut off my long braid.

I did not know vere I vould sleep. This running away is scary, I decided. I vas totally out of my element. There were no barns in town to slip into and sleep with cows. I saw house lights coming on, could smell suppers being cooked, and it made my stomach growl. I opened my duffel bag and lifted out a hard-boiled egg, savoring what might be my last egg from my chickens I cared for since hatchlings.

I vas missing the farm and comfort of my room with down mattress and quilt. But, nah, I vill not go back. Papa is probably so mad at me, I vould not be velcome to cross his threshold ever again. I vatched the sun go down, drawing my cloak tightly around me. With all those layers of clothing, I vasn't cold. But anxiety vas setting in. That is when man named Tony, wearing police uniform, asked if I needed help. He vas kind to me. Then, Preacher Kennedy came. They are like angels I heard about.

*****

She visualized angels coming to help to put her mind at ease so she could relax enough to sleep. Sometime after midnight, Martha slept to be awakened by the rising sun, not a rooster crowing. She said her morning prayers of thanksgiving for her good fortune and many blessings, dressed, drank a glassful of strange-tasting milk from a paper carton, and went down to see what lessons she would learn today in her new life.

Martha was a quick learner. She followed Carol around, anticipating what needed to be done. It wasn't long until she was very proficient at making beds to the Health Department standards, with the bathrooms sparkling, and Carol was learning from Martha how to use more natural products. Martha was also a marvelous cook. Carol was happy to have her, paid her a fair wage, and took her along to church services on Sundays, introducing her to the town folk. She was such a welcome addition to the household. Carol enjoyed having someone around who was the same age as her daughter Roberta.

Martha was able to find other odd jobs. She was doing some house sitting and pet sitting when people went out of town, walking some pets at lunchtime for people who worked away from Lucerne. However, she always made sure to be available if Carol needed help of any kind. She was sorry to decline when Carol invited her to share Christmas with the Webster family.

41

TOGETHERNESS

Christmas was approaching when Rob announced he was inviting a special guest to share Christmas weekend with the family. Would Carol please prepare an extra room? Due to uncertain weather, he would drive from Virginia instead of flying the Bonanza, so they wouldn't need to be picked up at the airport. Jim also asked if their reservations were clear so he could invite a weekend guest.

Carol was fine with extra people around. She was finally able to put her past in the past, letting go of old insecurities. Changing her name back to Webster helped. She was enjoying taking care of others in need of rest and relaxation. Their bookings were rewarding all fall, getting the business off to a great start. She had no reservations for Christmas weekend since she blocked the weekend for family time. Most people were going to warmer climates or staying home with family for the holidays. Besides, family will always take precedence over income.

Carol and Jim went up to the dusty attic and found a box marked Christmas Decorations. Inside, they found all their handmade, childhood ornaments. They laughed and had a good time with all the memories they shared. A few tears were shed too, but they finally got the large Scotch pine tree decorated with those treasures and strings of popcorn and paper chains of green-and-red construction paper for old times' sake. Wreaths of greens-with-red bows were hung in each window, and silver garlands were strung along porch railings. An inflatable teddy bear sat on the porch to greet guests and passersby.

Webster House was totally prepared for guests. The old family piano was tuned in case one of her brothers' guests wanted to play. She and Martha made up the necessary rooms and prepared a few casseroles for the freezer so she could be free to enjoy her family time. Martha worked several part-time jobs around town but was still staying in the garage apartment Jim wasn't anxious to move into. There were already quite a few advanced reservations for spring. Perhaps Martha would be full time soon.

The two women worked well together. Carol liked Martha and was feeling blessed for the way she came into their lives. She was a hard worker and didn't share much about her life before coming to Lucerne. Carol knew, over time, Martha would feel comfortable enough around her to open up. Carol wanted Martha to share Christmas with the family. However, Martha had a house-sitting job.

On December 24, Jim's guest arrived just as the first heavy snowfall of the season began. Jim went out to meet her at her car and then stomped his feet to clear his shoes of quickly accumulating snow. He barely let go of a fur-wrapped petite person with him. Opening the door, he called, "Carol, come meet Melissa."

Carol was already on her way down from an upstairs room where she watched them walking from her car to the porch. She never saw Jim being so gracious. Although Jim's guest was barely visible with all her wraps, Carol welcomed her. "Hello, Melissa. I'm Carol, Jim's sister. Welcome to Webster House. Please let me take your coat."

Jim helped Melissa with her coat, scarf, hat, and boots until she was visible. Petite and lovely, raven hair, button nose, clear and milky skin, dressed in a winter-white pantsuit, Melissa almost whispered, "Thank y'all so much. I lived and taught elementary school music in a little town in Alabama. I am still getting used to cold weather. Please forgive me, y'all. I am on sabbatical from my teaching job, currently working on my master's degree in music at IUP. That is Indiana University of Pennsylvania. When I say Indiana University, people think the state of Indiana. This is a great university, right here handy to my brother's family in Maryland. I have enjoyed spending time with my brother and nieces."

Carol bit her tongue to keep from smiling. "How did you two meet?" she asked while her back was turned to hang their coats in the foyer coat closet.

Melissa drawled, "Well, Jimmy was a friend of Danny, my brother, when they were both in the Navy. We met many years ago when I visited Danny at the base in Norfolk, Virginia. Danny called Jimmy a while ago when he was sick and wanted some company. He came to see Danny in Maryland while I was there too. Thankfully, my brother is recovering nicely. Isn't Jimmy the sweetest guy you've ever known? I could squeeze him to pieces."

Carol thought this was, indeed, going to turn out to be a fascinating Christmas. "Yes, *Jimmy* is certainly sweet. I'm so glad you could come spend time with us. Make yourself comfortable. *Jimmy*, why don't you show your guest to her room? I put her in the Maple Room." She excused herself and went to the kitchen to make some warming hot chocolate, smiling all the way.

Jim picked up Melissa's suitcase and led her to her room and showed her around the house before joining Carol in the kitchen to keep her company. Lunch was being prepared since Rob and his guest were due to arrive any minute. Melissa helped by setting the table for five in the large, eat-in kitchen where family loved to gather. The dining room table was already set for Christmas dinner tomorrow.

More snow had fallen before there was more foot stomping on the porch by Rob and his guest to rid their shoes of accumulating snow. Rob picked up the shovel from the side of the door and cleared the porch steps and sidewalk. His guest stood in the lawn, attempting to make snowballs, pelting Rob as he shoveled. Then, there was more stomping of feet before entering, hanging up coats, and going to the kitchen to join the rest of the family.

"Hey, gang. Say hello to Heidi. Heidi, this is my sister Carol, brother Jim, and hello there, I am Rob," he said, reaching out and shaking hands with Melissa. "I met Heidi on my skiing trip to Sweden last month. She is a flight attendant with Delta Airlines."

"How do you do," Heidi added with a deep voice and strong German accent. There were handshakes and hugs all around before everyone settled down to mugs of hot chocolate with marshmallows, barbecued ham sandwiches, and home fries. In spite of all their differences, conversation flowed smoothly.

Heidi revealed her father was retired from lignite mining in Leipzig, Germany. He managed to avoid contracting black lung, but coal mines were closed by 2018 according to government decree. "Yah, he vas hard vorker. My…how you say… Grundpa, vas also miner. We have lots in commun."

Melissa's voice was so soft, everyone practically had to hold his or her breath to hear. "My Papa is a retired miner living in Brookwood, Alabama, outside of Birmingham. We worried ourselves sick when we thought he had lung cancer. Bless his heart. He just caught a bad cold. He is doing fine again."

Randy came over after dinner. Carol wasn't sure how this would all turn out knowing animosity still existed between Rob and Randy. After some greetings and introductions and during a lull in conversation, Randy asked Carol, "Do you mind if I play your piano?"

"Please do. None of us play it. I didn't know you did. It has been tuned, and I dust it every week to honor my grandmother who played for church services long ago before your mother came to town. Some of the guests enjoy it. Here I thought you were total jock. When did you learn to play piano?"

"Oh, my mother treasured her Steinway grand. Dad always joked that the piano was her dowry. Mother planned to move it after she found a place to live. When she died, I got it by default. Neither of my sisters have room for it in their homes, nor could I see it just gathering dust and holding family photos. I got out my childhood lesson books and refreshed myself on long-forgotten skills as entertainment on long winter evenings over the last few years. I gave up practicing piano as a teenager when I realized playing sports was my ticket into college.

"I am sorry, Rob, but I needed it as badly as you did. After working in the mines for one summer, I could see the unfairness of the way miners were being treated. I felt all they needed was an attorney on their side. It nearly broke Mother's heart when I stopped playing the piano although she said she understood my desire for college. I'm not that good, but music seems appropriate tonight." He made himself comfortable on the bench.

Rob got up and looked out the window to check snow depth. When he came back to his chair, he gave Randy a dirty look and said nothing, but Carol could see he was still upset with Randy. Rob leaned over to elbow Carol and whispered, "Show-off."

Randy surprised them all by playing Christmas carols while they gathered around and sang. Melissa had a sweet soprano voice, Heidi added a strong alto, and Jim sang tenor. Rob hung back for a while but gradually joined the family at the piano, adding his bass. The sound of harmonizing voices reached far beyond the comfortable room with its tall tree decorated with ornaments saved over the growing-up years of the siblings. Randy scooted over for Carol to sit on the edge of the piano bench, sing soprano, turn pages, and make suggestions as to what to sing next, conferring with Randy if he could handle that many sharps or flats.

Both Jim and Carol, as local business owners, were honored when asked to do scripture readings for their church's Nativity production later that evening. When the ladies went upstairs to freshen up, Heidi offered to do a quick upsweep hairstyle for Carol when she changed out of her standard jeans into her long Christmas-green dress.

Randy was speechless as he watched Carol glide gracefully down the staircase. They all bundled up to go to Christmas Eve services at Fellowship Presbyterian Church, trooping up the sidewalk with Jim's arm tightly around Melissa's shoulders, Carol and Randy holding hands, and Rob and Heidi tossing snowballs at each other.

Carol never saw Jim so distinguished and sure of himself as when he walked to the pulpit for his turn at reading his part of the scripture. When it came time for Carol's reading, she walked to the pulpit and looked out over a church full of people. There wasn't room for everyone to sit in pews. People were standing in the back and along the sides. She choked up when she looked at her family sitting there in a row.

It was so beautiful and heartwarming to see everyone together. She missed Ma and Dad. She wished she could tell them that they were all getting along, doing things together. Her gaze fell on Pastor and Mrs. Kennedy in the front row, and she wanted to tell him she couldn't go on. However, seeing his friendly smile and an assuring nod telling her all was okay, she started her reading, swallowing a lump in her throat, and calming her quivering voice: "And it came to pass..."

After church, they went back to Webster House to be warmed by the fireplace before Randy left for his home. With hands covering yawns, everyone except Carol went to their respective rooms.

Carol made sure the coffee pot was programmed to start perking by six thirty and slipped back into the living room to place her wrapped packages under the tree and to fill five stockings she and Jim hung on the fireplace mantle a week ago. With an orange in the toe, topped with chocolate cream drops and new toothbrushes (something Ma did each year), she placed candy canes to stick out of the top.

Before turning off the tree lights, she reflected on what a joyous time this was. She was at home in Lucerne, where she was feeling totally comfortable in her new role as innkeeper. If only Ma and Dad could see them now. She was missing playing Santa for her daughters yet knew they were establishing their own lives. Roberta was visiting with potential in-laws, and Susie was on tour in England with her college choir.

Morning came quickly. Rob excused himself, shoveled his way to his car, and brought in mounds of packages, both his and Heidi's.

Jim brought a laundry basket full of packages he must have squirreled away in his upstairs closet since Martha was still staying in the garage apartment. Melissa asked, "Jimmy, could you get my packages from my trunk? I just love buying and wrapping presents. Thanks, y'all, for inviting me."

Such a grand time they all had opening packages, tossing wrapping papers into the center of the room where Penny played peekaboo and jumped with glee after flying ribbons.

All was going well until Randy dropped by to say Merry Christmas and give Carol a small package containing a necklace with an opal pendant, her birthstone. Carol took a risk and invited him to stay for Christmas dinner.

Rob motioned for Carol to go to the back porch rather than openly object. Once the door closed, he growled, "Here I thought we were going to have a family day, Carol. Do you have to invite this traitor?"

Carol gave Rob her sternest look. "Let's not spoil this day, all right? How can you say something like that when both Jim and you brought total strangers to share our family home? I welcomed them without any hesitation. Robert Clair, I'm going to say this once, and then we are going to finally put this to rest. Randy has apologized over and over and over. Didn't you hear him last night? However, he doesn't need to apologize to you, me, or anyone else. He needed a college scholarship as much as you did. You have too much to be thankful for to hold on to this grudge.

"He did not steal your scholarship. He earned it fair and square. You can't hold him responsible when you didn't quite measure up to the requirements. You can't always get through life on your good looks and blue eyes, you know. Now, you go back in there and behave yourself. Randy looked after Ma and Jim when you and I were ignoring them. He has been a true friend to me. We all owe him a debt of gratitude, and I am not going to let you spoil my chance at happiness if our relationship comes to that. I really don't know where our relationship is headed, but you better get used to having Randy around family gatherings." She clamped her mouth closed in a firm line, fists on her hips, and stared him down.

Rob was shocked. Carol never called him Robert Clair. Only Ma called him Robert Clair when she was disciplining him. He took a brief time to calm down and assess her words. In addition, he had to respect Carol was really the head of Webster House. He must admit Randy won the scholarship fair and square. Finally, he broke the silence and the stare down.

"You are so right, sis. I thought I was going to win based on my athletic ability. I forgot academic achievement was part of the scoring. Randy had the highest academic grades of any of the athletes, including me. He was smart, good-looking, strong, and an all-round nice guy. I hate to admit it, but I have been wrong about him for too long. I think I was jealous of his popularity and people skills. But you gotta admit, I am better looking!" he teased as he gave her a huge grin and peck on the cheek. "I'll behave, I promise. Just don't call me Robert Clair again. You sounded so much like Ma, I thought she was standing there beside you."

Carol had no choice but to chuckle and punch him playfully on his arm as they went back to join the others. Melissa was sitting on Jim's lap wrapped up in one of Ma's Afghans to keep warm. Heidi was telling everyone about growing up in Germany, herding sheep, and knitting wool sweaters to sell to tourists. Rob went over and clapped Randy on the back and added his own invitation for Randy to stay for Christmas dinner.

Carol looked out the window in time to see a sunray sparkle on new-fallen snow. She couldn't help but feel her mother's presence somehow. "Ma, if you are looking over us now, thanks and Merry Christmas."

After seeing to the remaining details, adding another place at the table for Randy, they all sat down to traditional stuffed turkey, mashed potatoes, candied sweet potatoes, cranberry sauce, Waldorf salad, Aunt Ethel's lime Jell-O salad, followed by pumpkin or apple pie with whipped cream or ice cream as toppings.

Later, after the dishwasher was purring quietly in the kitchen, they got an early start in talking about their individual resolutions for the upcoming New Year.

Rob said, "I want life to continue just as it is."

Jim looked down at Melissa and added, "God give me the wisdom to make good decisions in what I hope is a bright future."

Heidi added, "I am going to complete my American citizenship."

"I want to finish my master's degree and make positive changes in education," Melissa added before looking lovingly up at Jim.

Randy deferred to Carol to speak first.

Carol, with head bowed, said, "Thank you, God, for the blessings of this past year. May we use this special year to grow in our faith, make good decisions, and find peace."

42

DANGER

In March, Rob and his friend Heidi wanted to take advantage of his vacation time to travel to New Zealand. He contacted his sister Carol and brother Jim to see if they needed him for a few weeks.

"Go on, enjoy yourself. Everything is running smoothly with the B&B. Not much business to worry about," they assured him. "You can keep in touch with email. Take lots of pictures."

They saw the sights, experienced the friendliness of folks down under, and were on their way back home when the aircraft they were on developed a vibration. Flying over the South Pacific is not conducive to finding landing places, especially with a Lockheed L-1011 loaded with ninety-seven people. The cockpit crew knew Captain Robert Webster, a company check pilot, was traveling with a companion in first class.

The copilot called for the head flight attendant to enter the cockpit area, advised her of their situation, and asked her to please not cause alarm but to ask Captain Webster to come forward. Another set of eyes, ears, and his years of experience would be advantageous. They advised her to tell him, "There is a monkey loose in the cargo bay," which is code for "we have a major problem needing assistance."

Rob calmly left his seat next to Heidi and used his secret number code to enter the cockpit. "What's up, guys?" But he already knew they had a problem as he was feeling the vibration.

"Thanks for coming up, captain. The augmented crew is sleeping. Rather than break their rest time, maybe you could help out? Seems we have a vibration. All engine instruments are reading normal. What do you think? And do you have any alternate ideas, other places to make a cautionary landing before reaching our Honolulu destination?"

"Give me a minute to make some assessment and organize my thoughts. One thing I have learned is never to act in haste. First off, you guys fly the plane. Too many accidents are caused by distraction of dealing with a problem and forgetting to maintain control of the aircraft."

Rob took the copilot's headset and started talking to the company and doing some old-fashioned flight planning. He remembered having a problem back in his military flying days when they landed on a remote island where NASA had a tracking station and historical prominence as a stay-over point back in the days of Pan American's Clipper flying boats. He pinpointed the location of Canton Island, an atoll in the Phoenix Islands, in relation to where they were. However, that runway was short, and Fiji was closer. "The best thing to do is to get this baby on the ground ASAP, then figure out what to do next. The goal here is to save the SOBs [souls on board]." Of course, he was rather determined to also survive this situation.

He checked runway length at Fiji and determined it could handle an aircraft of this size and weight. He called on 123.9, "United 220, we have a situation up here, requesting diversion to your runway and vectors for your location."

"Roger, United 220, we understand your need. Turn to a heading of 330. We have you on long-range radar at 200 miles. Continue your approach and descend. Expect further vectors."

Rob calculated their rate of descent, staying higher than normal in case an engine failed. He advised the company where they were diverting, and the company advised they would get a maintenance crew headed their direction from Honolulu when advised they were safely on the ground.

Rob walked back to his seat to let Heidi know he would be in the cockpit for landing, but there was nothing to worry about. "Read your book. We are diverting to take care of this monkey. We will be back in the air before you know it." The neighboring passengers heard his calm voice and were comforted.

The vibration was increasing. The emergency checklist was completed, and descent continued. Seeing Fiji emerge out of all that water beneath them was a thrill. He wondered, as he often did, how Amelia Earhart must have felt when she searched and searched for tiny Howland Island and never found it. He had a quick thought of Carol and the enjoyment he was having being part of the family venture. He uttered a quick prayer for his safe return and, of course, the rest of the passengers. However, this was not a time to let his mind wander.

He sat down, buckled into the jump seat, and monitored instruments and handled communications. Echo Intersection was reported, and the aircraft was maintaining a high glide slope for Runway 34. Using their best short-field procedures, touch down was smooth. They were met with fire trucks and every piece of emergency equipment available on this remote location. Rob breathed a sigh of relief they were not needed. They were led to a small terminal to offload passengers, most of them unaware of any problem.

The passengers were given snacks and drinks as the base manager tried to entertain until the length of their stay could be determined. Meanwhile, he was locating housing for them, just in case. They found space for the men and women, which would fill every available resort cabana on the island paradise. They would have to manage with what few items they had in carry-on luggage rather than offload suitcases from cargo to cause delay should the problem be rectified quickly. The cargo door was opened as a ruse of catching the loose monkey. There were all kinds of jokes going around about someone not fastening the monkey's cage.

As it turned out, there was a skeleton United maintenance crew on the island, and the aircraft was towed to a maintenance building, where a loose cowling latch was discovered and suspected of being the cause of the vibration. Just to be safe, the cowling was opened to determine there was nothing obviously wrong with the engine itself. The cowling was closed and securely latched. A ground run-up was performed with no further vibration.

By the time the correction was made, estimated crew duty time was exceeded before their destination would be reached. They chose to spend the night and depart early the next morning. The passengers and crew were bussed to their accommodations. There was not much to do in Fiji except loll around on the beach or beside the pool. The beach was attractive, except sharks were swimming just offshore. They were warned to not leave the resort grounds after dark. A party atmosphere existed, and no one knew how close he or she came to being on the news back home.

In fact, when Rob and Heidi returned home, no one knew they returned a day late. That was one thing Rob appreciated about not living in Lucerne. He did what he wanted when he wanted. He didn't want to tell Carol about the experience for her protection. She would worry like Ma used to do.

43

DISCOVERY

One mild spring day, Martha was walking a client's Schnauzer in town when the friendly truck driver from her past turned the corner and stopped in front of The Company Store. Her papa was with him. She watched as he got out of the truck and headed for the store. She debated what to do, so she simply sat down on the bench in front of Bloomers to gather her thoughts.

Jim was at the cash register when the truck driver and a thin, bearded man wearing all black and a beat-up hat came into the store through the open door. "Young man, I am looking for my runaway daughter. She goes by Mart'a. She is plain looking, long braid hanging down back, or wrapped around head. Have thee seen her? This man say he left her in this town ven delivering quilts and such."

Jim thought for a minute. "Yes, there was a young woman meeting that description in here quite a while ago. She must be a quilter. She was helpful with naming quilt patterns on quilts I sell on consignment. But I haven't seen her since. She left when the truck driver did and hasn't come back."

"She did not return home. Driver doesn't know anything more. Just gave him a note she wrote for storekeeper to give to me next time I go to store. Oh vell, no big loss. I have new vife. Daughter disobedient, vouldn't do vat I promise. Danke, anyvay." He stomped toward the door of The Company Store. "Nah, she did not return to her home." And he walked outside and headed toward the delivery truck.

Jim puzzled over the man's question for a moment, then ignored the whole incident until he saw Martha walking toward the man. Something about her profile reminded him of the daughter this man was seeking. Jim watched out the front window as Martha approached the bearded man. "Hmm. Could that be the Mart'a he asked about? That would explain a lot." He chuckled as he watched to see what would happen.

Out on the sidewalk, Martha approached Papa and the truck driver, wondering if he would recognize her in her new clothes and hairstyle. "Excuse me, did I hear you are looking for someone?" she asked.

Her papa looked right at her and answered, "No, miss, I am looking for my old-maid daughter who ran away last fall. Have you seen a plain-looking woman with long hair made up in braids?" He hesitated a moment then frowned and asked, "Mart'a, is that thee? Have thee gone mad to cut your hair and dress so wickedly? No daughter of mine would do such a t'ing to shame me and my family."

Martha stood in front of her father and said, "Yes, Papa, I am Martha. I have come to my senses. No more braids. No more old maid name-calling. I have created a new life here in Lucerne. I have jobs to earn money. I have nice place to live. I have friends who care about me, and I go to a nice church. I know you will now shun me, but it doesn't matter anymore. I am a decent person in spite of what you think of me. I am never going back to farm life and your narrow-minded way of thinking and believing you have preached to me all my life. I cannot abide by men making all the rules, or women not having say-so in anything. Here, I am happy. I am respected. I still love you and my family. However, unless you can accept me the way I have become, then I must say goodbye." She turned and started to walk away with Scruffy following closely.

"Mart'a, please."

Martha turned back to face her father.

"Let me tell thee. I have married Louisa, and Harvey Brinkerhoff has found a mate in Velma Goodnight. You remember? She vas widow with three babes of her own. They will marry next wedding season. I wish thee well. At least I found thee, and thee is safe and happy."

The truck driver stood by and watched this exchange with a puzzled expression on his face. After Papa stomped off to get back in the delivery truck, the driver gave Martha a thumbs-up signal, a nod of approval, and walked toward his truck.

Jim watched this exchange through his front window. "Now it all adds up," he said to his friend Randy, who happened to be in the store at the time. "She is a runaway from the Amish. I remember her now. Well, no matter. I am still glad she came to town. Carol would be lost without her."

44

THE FUTURE

For a while, Jim held off proposing to Melissa. He rationalized to himself, *I'm not getting any younger. I need to act before Melissa's semester is over so she doesn't go back to Alabama to teach school.* He did not want to marry before Carol and Randy figured out their relationship. However, they weren't making any progress. Both were too busy in their own lives to spend much time together. Carol wasn't thrilled about Randy's flying or being away as much as he needed to be to take care of his out-of-state clients.

Carol was happy for Jim when he told her of his intentions. Of all people, he deserved to be happy. "Jim, if you want, you could build a house on the farm's western corner."

On a lovely end-of-March evening, Jim took Melissa's hand in his. "Melissa, sweetie, I don't want you to go back to Alabama. I want you to stay here with me on our farm and be my wife. I would be so honored if you would accept my offer of love for the rest of our lives."

"Jimmy, I thought you would never ask. Yes, yes! I'd love to be your wife and become part of your family. I have loved you for so long. I can get a job here at the school. I already asked for an interview."

Jim immediately started making some initial drawings to show his fiancée when she came to visit on weekends and quickly sent an email asking Jonathan if he would put them on his construction schedule. When he told Carol about Jonathan agreeing to be their builder, she remembered the feelings she once had for this stranger who came into her life so unexpectedly, then was gone just as stronger feelings for him surfaced. How would she feel having him nearby for the length of time it took to build Jim and Melissa's new house? She could not make any promises to Randy until she had time to explore which man meant more to her.

Jim was totally involved in the design of a new house. In order to please Melissa, he wanted their house to look good in Pennsylvania and add some traditional Southern plantation columns. He didn't want to overshadow the B&B either. He would go to Williamstown next Sunday with his rough draft to get Jonathan's input. Perhaps he could invite him here for Sunday dinner. He would check with Carol.

Carol really didn't have time to think about Jim's or Rob's or anyone's problem but her own. That morning, she received a call from the hospital to have her mammogram repeated. "Darn it all. Ma had this problem. Am I doomed to have the same life pattern?"

She made an appointment for a repeat mammogram then worried until the day of the retest about whether any man would ever love her if she lost her breasts. Would she feel like a total woman ever again? After her mammogram was read, they followed up with an ultrasound. She went home and waited for a call the next day from her doctor. She spent another night of wondering and worrying.

She nearly jumped out of her shoes the next morning when the phone rang. Seeing the doctor's number on the call ID, she sat down and took an extra deep breath before answering. "Hello, Carol Webster of Webster House," she said hesitantly.

"Miz Webster, I have good news and bad news. The good news is that you don't have anything to worry about at this time. The bad news is, we want you to have another mammogram in six months to be sure. The condition you have is fibrocystic breast disease. This can sometimes become a problem, but you are still young. We want you to stay vigilant and repeat your mammogram every six months for the next two years just to keep a watch on anything developing. It might help if you cut down on caffeine. Other than that, enjoy life. Keep your weight down, exercise, and don't worry."

She breathed a sigh of relief, not realizing she had been holding her breath while listening to the doctor's report. She realized she wanted to talk to someone about this problem. Since Randy was her best friend at the time, she picked up the phone to call him just as she heard a car pull into the driveway. She didn't want an interruption right now. However, she was a businesswoman and couldn't ignore a potential guest. She opened the door to find Randy standing on the porch with a worried look on his face.

"Jim told me you had some tests…" He didn't finish his greeting since Carol was smiling.

Carol took his hand and they walked together into the living room where she shared her good news and said, "Everything is just fine, Randy. As fine as it could be. Thanks for coming by." She gave him the details of all the tests and results. "I feel I have a second chance at a new life. I'm glad we share this special friendship. I needed to share my good news and there you were when I needed someone."

"You know I'll always be here for you," Randy said with a hint of regret that he couldn't be there all the time as he would prefer.

45

NEW FRIENDSHIP

Martha was supervising Webster House one Tuesday while Carol was at the in-town office. A guest went out to his car and accidentally locked his keys inside. "I think Carol has called Constable Tony before under this situation. Let me see what he can do." Martha called an emergency number posted next to the telephone and left a message with the county dispatcher.

Before long, there was a knock on the door. Martha opened the door to a tall smiling man. His uniform and name tag spoke for itself, identifying him as the constable she called. She also recognized him as the lawman watching over her in the park many months ago when she first arrived in town. The shock of seeing him again brought back her memory of sitting alone and scared on the park bench. Evidently, he didn't remember her since she looked so different now with her hair cut short and modern clothing instead of so many layers of farm clothing.

"Hello. My name is Tony. I am here to see someone needing help with some keys locked inside their car."

She motioned to the young couple sitting in the living room. "Thank you for coming so quickly."

"Not much goes on in this quiet town, not during the day at least. Glad to be of assistance." He talked to the young couple but kept glancing back at her. He went out to their locked car, used a special tool he carried in the patrol car, and their door was opened in no time at all. The young couple got in their car and drove away. Tony walked up onto the porch where Martha was standing. "You can call me anytime you have a problem. I'm happy to help. Have we met before?"

She didn't know exactly how to answer but felt honesty was the best policy. "I met you briefly when I was new to town." But she didn't tell him exactly when or where.

"Oh okay. I guess I have seen you with Carol and Jim around town. There aren't a lot of young people around here since most moved away to find greener pastures. Would you like to join our church bowling team? We meet on Tuesday evenings and go out for dessert after." He could see she seemed interested, and he felt he was talking too fast in his eagerness to spend more time with her.

"Sure. I would like that. I have never gone bowling but wouldn't mind learning," she answered.

"I will pick you up and introduce you to the others. Is 6:45 okay? Newcomers are always welcome." He tipped his cap and smiled as he went back to work patrolling the quiet streets of Lucerne.

Promptly at 6:45 that evening, Tony arrived. Martha was sitting on the porch swing waiting for him. They drove to the bowling alley where he oversaw her shoe rental, selected a bowling ball appropriate to her size, and introduced her to the rest of the group. Some she recognized from church. Tony seemed different out of uniform.

He carried his height well. His blue eyes with flecks of brown were captivating. He was clean-shaven, which was probably a requirement for his job. He also looked friendlier out of uniform and had a great sense of humor. She enjoyed his company so much, she didn't want the evening to end. Everyone trekked off to Isaly's Ice Cream parlor after bowling, which turned out to be fun. Martha never before enjoyed an evening so much in her life.

When they got back to Webster House, she let him know she lived in the upstairs apartment. He walked her to the garage's side entrance and asked, "Would you like to go bowling again? Or maybe you would enjoy a movie?"

She didn't really know how to answer; she looked into his eyes and simply nodded. He reached out and took her hand to hold in his. She felt happier than she ever felt before. "Before you go, I want to thank you for bringing Pastor Kennedy to my aid in the park when I ran away from my Amish farm life. I want to be honest with you about who I am."

"I see the resemblance now. I was concerned about you that night. Although not much happens in Lucerne to be concerned about, sleeping on a park bench is not good for anyone. The worse thing to happen would be a passing skunk." He stopped talking to chuckle. Her tinkling laugh was so attractive. He knew then a relationship with her could end his loneliness. He was still holding her hand, which he used to bring her closer to him. He whispered in her ear, "See you tomorrow, and every day if you will let me."

She coyly smiled and accepted a gentle kiss on her cheek.

46

JONATHAN SEEKS ANSWERS

Each morning when Jonathan arrived to work on Jim and Melissa's house construction, he looked hopefully at Webster House. He wanted to see Carol. Although she was friendly back in October at the wedding for their opening weekend, she was avoiding being close to him. The first evening he came to see Jim and Melissa to review their plans, she served coffee and fresh apple pie then excused herself to spend the rest of the evening in her office, keeping her distance. On several mornings, when he stopped to pick up Jim at Webster House, Carol came out and gave a friendly wave before turning around to quickly walk back inside. If only he could find an excuse to spend quality time with her.

He and Jim were going over a minor construction change suggestion from Melissa one morning when Carol walked into what would eventually be the kitchen. "Hi there, guys. Would one of you please look into why my car won't start this morning? No hurry if I can use your Bronco today, Jim. I need to go to a chamber meeting, and this late cold snap is just too cold for me to walk into town. I need a few groceries too."

"I need to pick up some supplies for Jonathan," Jim replied. "Jonathan, could I do that later this afternoon?"

Jonathan saw his opening. "Carol, you can certainly take my truck. I will be working here all day, and it is just going to be sitting there. When I take my lunch break, I'll walk over and take a look at your Fusion," he said with a smile and polite nod.

Carol responded, "That would be so kind of you. I promise to take good care of your truck."

He walked her to his truck to remove some tools he might need when he checked her car. "If the car has been running well up to this time, it is probably something simple. I'll check it over. I know a few things about cars. My brother and I started his service station together. We used to work on antique cars. I left after just a year when my Uncle Merle wanted help in his construction company. Harrison Construction was his until he passed away. That's when I took over his company." He handed Carol his truck keys, and their fingers touched for an instant. She looked up at him, acting startled. However, she took his keys, turned, got in the truck, and drove away. Again, she saw in the rearview mirror that he watched as she drove away.

While driving his truck, she wondered to herself why she was avoiding him. *He is only being a friend. He was as much a victim of my husband's infidelity as I was.* She enjoyed driving his truck, being close to his belongings, taking in the scent of his aftershave lingering in the upholstery. *Am I being fair to him? Or myself? What I have with Randy is comfortable. Shouldn't there be something more in a relationship? Am I settling for comfort when Jonathan might bring excitement?*

Carol had a hard time keeping her mind on the chamber of commerce meeting she attended. She kept rubbing her fingers that seemed to spark when they touched his. She was thinking about all the what-ifs. *What if Jonathan and Jacob were not behind me on Dulles Highway? If they were in front of me, they would not have known I needed help, and we would have never met. What if my car had not broken down that day? Was this a case of divine intervention? Am I wrong to be ignoring this opportunity to find love again? Although Randy and I are an item, no promises were made, no dates set. My ring finger is still bare. God, give me answers. Is this thy will?"*

She went from the chamber meeting to Kroger, idly wandering up and down food aisles, wondering what it was she needed, picking up a box or can, reading the label, and putting it back on the shelf.

She checked her watch and figured Jonathan could possibly be at Webster House checking her car at that precise moment. She quickly selected some lunch items, checked out, and rushed home.

The garage door was open, and both Jim and Jonathan were bent over the engine compartment of Ma's car, now hers. She tried to act casual. "Have you found the problem yet?"

Jonathan was reading a gauge he held in his hand. "Just as I thought. This cold weather has affected your battery. I will put a charger on it and check it again before I go home. But you might think about getting a new battery. Based on the car being almost seven years old, I'd say it is time for a new one anyway."

Jim commented, "Ma took good care of her car, but I don't know of her havin' any problems with startin' or buyin' a battery. She would have asked me to do that for her."

Jonathan looked at her and smiled his sweetest, dimple-revealing smile when their eyes met. She swallowed hard to get her heart back down and out of her throat. *If only he wouldn't stand so close. If only my heart didn't start thumping when he smiles that way.* Taking a few steps toward the kitchen door, she had an inspiration. "I bought some cold cuts for lunch. Let me fix you a sandwich and some hot soup before you go back to work. Then how about supper when you check the battery later?"

Jonathan looked pleased as he politely accepted both invitations. He could hardly believe he was going to be able to spend some time with her. "What can I bring?"

"Just bring yourself. You are working hard to make a beautiful home for Jim and Melissa. This is a thank-you for working so hard, checking my car, and for being a good friend. Oh, and I put your truck keys above the driver's visor. Thanks for letting me borrow it. Let me make those sandwiches. Come in when you are finished." She hurried inside to get out of the cold and calm herself.

When the guys went back to work after lunch, Carol spent the afternoon fixing a special supper. She changed out of her jeans and sweatshirt and put on a skirt and blouse with matching cardigan sweater. The guys came in with ruddy cheeks from working in the cold and quickly washed up at the basement sink since their meal was ready. After they ate, complimenting Carol on how good her chicken pot pie tasted, Jim went to his room to call Melissa to tell her Jonathan made her requested changes in the kitchen layout.

While he was gone, Carol and Jonathan quickly loaded the dishwasher and had time to play a game of Scrabble at the dining room table and talk, mostly about the new house. However, the longer they talked, the more she realized they had a strong connection. Although there was also a strong attraction, there was a barrier standing between them that wouldn't go away. She saw pain in his eyes when he looked at her; he saw the same pain reflected in hers. They would always be connected to each other through the tragedy of her husband's death.

Jim came back downstairs, and the guys started talking about work plans for the next day. Carol slipped quietly back into the kitchen to prepare for tomorrow's breakfast. Jonathan went into the kitchen to say goodbye and gave her a tender hug and a lingering kiss on the cheek. "You know I really care for you, don't you, Carol?"

"Jonathan, I do. And I care for you too. If only…"

Jonathan stood back, lowered his head, and studied his shoes. "I know. You don't need to say it. I have conflicting thoughts regarding the past. I believe I can overlook the barrier that separates us. Can you?"

Carol admitted, "I honestly don't know. I feel we both have too much pain to ignore."

Jonathan reached out to take her hand. "Why did we find each other after all these years? Is this my punishment—to find you and not be allowed to experience love again?"

Carol picked up the dishcloth and wiped the counter, although it was already clean. "I'm not sure what we are both feeling is love or pity or empathy. I only know there is too much history. I am heartbroken our chance for happiness has been stolen from us. As much as I am tempted to try to put the past in the past, I know we will never be able to forget." Carol looked around the room, focusing on anything else except Jonathan's eyes.

"As much as it hurts, I do understand. I wish you all the happiness you can find with Randy or someone else who deserves you.

I only wish it could be me. If it doesn't work out and if you can ever find a way to forget or at least totally forgive, I'll be here." He reached out and put his arms around her, and she welcomed his embrace.

They stood there together until Carol almost changed her mind. He was such a gentleman, and a spark of passion was certainly present. She looked up at him, attempted a weak smile, and nearly whispered, "I'll certainly keep you in mind."

With another gentle kiss on her cheek, fighting the urge to stay and fight for what he wanted, he turned quickly and left, shaking hands with Jim as he went through the living room. "See you tomorrow," he said with a little catch in his voice.

Carol bustled around in the kitchen, swiping angrily at the hot tears rolling down her cheeks, washing away the feel of his kiss.

47

ANOTHER WEDDING

Jim and Melissa's house was completed, and their wedding day finally arrived. This was not only their wedding day, but after the ceremony at Webster House, their reception would be held at their own home as an open house. Jim, being a pillar in the community, posted an open invitation in the window of The Company Store to spend the afternoon in the fresh air and sunshine on their new back lawn. Landscapers finished their job just the week prior.

Carol was humming a tune about the sun shining on a happy bride as she served breakfast to family and guests as the day dawned bright and clear after an overnight rain. She spent the morning bustling about, going back and forth between the two houses on her new green golf cart, checking with caterers, flower deliveries, and the musical group's setup.

To gather the family together, Carol rang the bell Ma used to call them all in from playing. "Come, everyone. The photographer is here. We will do some of the family group photos now to make it less time consuming after the ceremony when we will want to be mingling with guests."

Pastor and Mrs. Kennedy arrived, followed by some early guests, including Jonathan. Carol tried to ignore his presence. However, she could sense his eyes following her, which was leaving her flustered, a feeling she could ill afford.

Jonathan wanted desperately to speak with her, so he offered to help. Instead of giving him a job near her, she suggested, "You could help by going out to the field being used for parking to help create some order in getting cars parked for ease of egress so no one gets blocked in." She was able to concentrate again on her tasks at hand without the distraction of his being so close. She kept watching out the window, though, seeing him in action while helping Tony establish a convenient parking arrangement.

Everyone gathered inside since it was damp under the rose arbor from the rain. Randy and Melissa's brother Danny, as ushers, seated family members and close friends in the living room. Carol and her daughters were seated in the front row before Melissa's parents were seated on the other side. Carol's thoughts were on the many changes over the past year. She moved from a lonely, barely existing life in Virginia to being a wealthy businesswoman and major property owner in her hometown. She was grateful for the family home being saved from a fire and Jim's transformation from Jimbo to Jim. If only she could resolve her conflict over the two men in her life.

Mrs. Trimble played the familiar "Wedding March" on the newly tuned piano. Melissa's sisters, Diana and Carla, preceded the bride to stand in front of the fireplace. Promptly at 1:28, Melissa descended the stairs in a cloud of white organdy, lace, and tulle. Almost all eyes were on the bride as she walked demurely to Jim, with Rob next to him as best man and Melissa's brother Danny standing next to Rob. However, Carol was watching Jim's chin quiver while trying to keep his tears from falling from his glistening brown eyes. Carol watched as her brother took on the responsibility of a wife, kissing Melissa tenderly at the appointed time.

After a few more photos, Randy held Carol's hand on the short walk across the field to the new home built by Jonathan and his crew. Such a lovely home it was. Everyone was admiring the finished product.

Carol was finally able to relax and let the caterers and musicians take over the rest of the day's activities. Randy accompanied Carol while circulating through the crowd, visiting with townsfolk. Jonathan was getting a lot of attention as builder of the house.

However, each time Carol glanced his way, he was looking at her. Each time their eyes met, he smiled or winked or gave a friendly little wave. Frequently, she found him standing nearby as he, too, was circulating around the lawn. She kept hearing his voice as he explained different aspects of the building process.

She lost sight of Randy and discovered Jonathan was directly in front of her, and they were alone on the edge of the crowd. "Carol, I need to talk to you."

"Right now? I can hardly leave my brother's reception," she curtly answered as she glanced around to see who was close enough to overhear their conversation.

"No, not right now," he said as he touched her left hand for an instant, noting there was still no ring. "But soon. When can you get away for an hour or two?"

"Tomorrow? Life should be calming down after today. The newlyweds will be off on their trip to Bermuda. Rob is flying Susie back to Penn State for her summer session. Roberta is driving back to Winchester. Melissa's parents will be leaving too. The remaining guests will checkout in the morning. I can get my work cleared up by late afternoon. Does that work for you?" she said while still scanning the crowd for eavesdroppers.

"How about dinner? You choose the restaurant, but it needs to be a place where we can talk—really talk. Plus, you need a break after all this commotion and all the work you did to make this the perfect wedding for one lucky couple. Do they realize how lucky they are?"

"Yes. They do seem perfect together. Jim knows how lucky he is, in more ways than one. Okay, I accept. Someone else's cooking would taste good about now," she agreed with a little chuckle.

"Be ready at 4:00 and we can have lots of time to talk and get you back to the B&B."

Just then, a wedding guest asked Jonathan, "What shade of stain was used on the trim work in the house?"

Jonathan began, "Well, I mix my own custom colors until I get what the customer wants. This is a combination of…"

Carol excused herself and went in search of Randy who was on the back porch, sitting on the railing looking out over the crowd.

He had loosened his tie and was beginning to relax until he saw the two of them together on the edge of the crowd. Unknown to her, he watched the exchange between Carol and Jonathan, taking note of the looks they exchanged. As a trial lawyer, he was aware of body language, facial expressions, and mannerisms revealing a person's inner psychological response to external stimuli. Even though he could not hear what was being said, he knew what he needed to know. The way she swayed toward him when he spoke and the way he touched her hand while she was speaking told him more than he wanted to admit.

She spoke to a few more people as she maneuvered across the lawn. Reaching the privacy of the porch, she sat down on the glider, relieved to be off her feet. Randy took her hand and asked, "Are you okay? You are shaking."

"I am all right. It's been a difficult day, watching my little brother marrying, acknowledging he is all grown up, with a wife, a home, and probably a family of his own soon. I will miss him at the house. But Melissa is such a doll. I will enjoy having a sister at long last." She started wondering to herself what Alice Faye would have been like had she lived.

The cake was cut and served to those who remained. When the single ladies were gathered together, Melissa looked directly at Carol before turning her back to the small group. Melissa's bouquet toss was pinpoint accurate directly into Carol's hands. She blushed as all applauded or pointed toward Randy.

Jonathan turned his back to keep his pained expression to himself. He walked to his car and slipped away while everyone watched Jim toss the bride's garter to Randy. He heard the cheering and didn't like it one bit.

Jim and Melissa changed into traveling clothes before a limousine whisked them away to the airport and two weeks of honeymooning. Carol let tears slip down her cheeks as she waved goodbye, blew kisses, and wished them more luck than she had in her marriage.

Randy waited patiently as she finished her hostess duties, and they walked together back across the field to the Webster House porch. "You seem lost in thought, Carol. Is there something you need to get off your mind? I am a good listener, you know."

"Oh Randy. I am not in the mood to talk right now. I think I need to take care of guests and have some quiet time and a nice hot tub before turning in. I still have a few guests staying over and breakfast to make for morning. Of course, Martha and Tony will help. I am bushed."

"Carol, if you don't want to talk, could I ask you to at least listen to me for a few minutes? I have been aware for some time of your conflict over whether to forgive Jonathan. You may not realize this, but I am also aware of your attraction to him. I had hoped, while listening to the vows exchanged between Jim and Melissa, you would be inspired to consider my marriage proposal of many months ago. The problem is, Carol, you were looking for Jonathan, not at me."

"Oh, Randy, not now, I—"

"Yes now, Carol. You see, I have been offered a federal magistrate judgeship in Harrisburg. I was going to turn down the position, although this is a huge honor. I want you to marry me. However, each time I bring it up, you aren't ready. Will you ever be ready, Carol? From what I observed today, you need to resolve whatever is going on between you and Jonathan. All I ask is for you to be honest with me but, more importantly, be honest with yourself.

"Now I will let you go, but think about what I said. I have a deadline on the judgeship offer. If you want me here in Lucerne, I'll stay, but only if you are ready to make a commitment to me for whatever time we have left. I know this is a lot to ask of you when you are so tired and emotionally drained. I did say last year I would be patient. I believe I have been. But I must have an answer within the next week. Say yes you'll marry me, and I'll stay since I know you would not be willing to leave Lucerne after what you have gone through this past year getting Webster House established. Otherwise, I have no choice but to move on with my life."

He took her in his arms, gently kissed her on her cheek, and then looked her in the eye. "We haven't talked much about love. I do love you, Carol. I hoped our relationship based on our friendship would be enough for you."

She started to speak, but he stopped her with a finger laid gently on her lips. "Don't say anything now. Give me a call when you can give me your honest answer." He turned away before she could say anything, got in his car, and left.

Carol sat on the porch swing for a long time, thinking about Randy's words before she changed from her dress into comfortable clothing to prepare for an early breakfast for departing guests. She said good night to Rob, Roberta, and Susan and went to her bedroom, kicked off her shoes, stretched out on the bed for a moment, and fell asleep in her clothes.

About three in the morning, Carol got up, slipped into her nightgown, eased herself under the covers, and lay awake in the dark for another hour pondering her dilemma. She did not have easy answers. Randy was pressuring her. Could she afford to lose his friendship? Her heart and her brain were fighting over choices she must make. She didn't want to hold him back from his opportunity, something probably every attorney in Pennsylvania dreamed about. *What was so urgent that Jonathan needed to say?* she wondered. After four more turns and two more pillow fluffings, she slept.

48

THE HONEST TRUTH

Carol completed the morning ritual of breakfast and checkout with the guests and made sure that Rob and her daughters took home some wedding cake after putting the top layer in the freezer for Jim and Melissa's anniversary next year. The last guests left at nine thirty. She then talked to herself as she went about her cleanup of Webster House and did laundry.

Why is Jonathan unhappy with the way things are? We are friends! Isn't that enough? Can I find it in my heart to totally forgive him? He doesn't know how much I have to offer him. He thinks I am only the owner of Webster House, and I share that with my brothers. How will he feel when I tell him I own half the town? I need to be upfront with him.

Martha helped make the cleanup of the B&B efficient and thorough. "Do you have plans for later?" Martha asked. "You seem to be in a rush to get things organized. Do you need me to cover for you if you are going out?"

"Oh, Martha, thanks. That would be so kind of you. Yes, I am going out to dinner with a friend. There's someone at the door. I'll see who it is. Keep the laundry going."

When she got to the door, there stood Randy. She wasn't eager to see him as her thoughts were on her dinner date with Jonathan. "Hi, Randy. Come on in. I'm sort of busy right now but always have time to take a break and talk with a friend."

"Carol, I stopped by to see if you wanted to go to church with me this morning and have lunch afterward so we could have more time to talk. About what you just said—we are friends, aren't we?"

"I really don't have time for church today with so much to do to get ready for the afternoon check-ins. I'm not sure what you mean by that question. Of course, we are friends, very good friends—special friends. That will never change."

"Is that all we are ever going to be? I want more than friendship, Carol. I asked you to think about making a life with me, not just deep, lasting friendship. As I told you last evening, but I know you might not realize how serious I am. I want a change from friendship to a loving relationship. When I saw you and Jonathan talking yesterday at the wedding reception, you were extra attentive to him. And yes, I notice now the blush on your cheeks when his name is mentioned. I am not blind. I can see where you are headed. I fear it's not down any aisle with me."

"Randy… I'm sorry. This is all so confusing. I really don't know what is happening. I was planning on marrying you after Webster House was up and running. After I met Jonathan and faced the effect he had on my life, I hated him. However, over time, for my own peace of mind, I had to forgive him for the accidental killing of Ted. Jonathan is as much a victim as I am by my husband's infidelity. Once I forgave him and faced the honest truth, I realized there is a special bond between us. He worked so hard to get Webster House ready. I care about him. What is the future like? I don't know. I will be honest with you and tell you I am having dinner with him this evening to talk. He requested this. I don't know why. That's what you saw us talking about yesterday after the wedding. Please try to understand. I feel I owe him his say."

Randy took her hand and leaned in to kiss her. She turned her head so the kiss fell on her cheek. "I'll wait to hear from you. You can call me later, if not too late."

"I need a little time to make a decision about your proposal, but I will get back to you with my answer as soon as I have made up my mind. If you choose to go to Harrisburg, I will miss you. Lucerne won't be the same without you here." Her gaze was traveling around the room, noting everything she needed to put in order. Her mind was not ready to make any firm decision about the future until she completed today's to-do list.

Randy gently held her chin so she looked him in the eye. "I love you and want you for my wife." However, Randy saw Carol's pained expression and knew she was not ready to respond. He released her and quietly let himself out the door, dejectedly crossing the porch and down the steps, walking to his car. He sat in his car for a few minutes to evaluate what just happened. He was on his way to church knowing he had a lot to pray about. Perhaps God will give him an answer.

Carol heard the door close as she hurried back to the laundry room with his repeat proposal heavy on her heart and mind. This was not a simple choice, certainly nothing she could solve by flipping a coin. This was her future. Marrying Randy meant ignoring her feelings for Jonathan. Not marrying Randy meant hurting someone she had known and loved a long time. *But do I have the right kind of love for him? I was wrong before. I don't want to make another mistake.*

Martha saw her worried expression. "Is there something you want to talk about while we work?"

"No. I have a decision to make, and I am not ready to make that decision. I am going to go by the old saying—*to not decide is to decide.* I need to take more time, and that's what I am going to do. Let's go upstairs and work our way down, but I'll straighten up the living room first."

49

DECISION TIME

Carol finished her work and took a long hot shower to soothe her aching muscles and calm her nerves. She was drying her hair when she realized how much Randy's morning visit upset her and added to her confusion. She couldn't assume anything or guess what Jonathan wanted to talk about. She was only trying to deal with her own emotions.

As she dressed in her favorite burgundy sundress, adding gray sandals, she checked her reflection in the mirror. Running the B&B was good for her. The dress fit better since she lost some weight. Writing kept her in a chair. The B&B kept her active. She went downstairs when she heard Martha greeting Jonathan, who arrived precisely on time.

"Good evening, Carol," he greeted her at the bottom of the stairs, already holding her light jacket in case the evening turned cool. "You look marvelous."

He was quite dashing in his gray slacks and burgundy polo shirt, as though they had planned their attire. "Nice to see you too, Jonathan."

He carefully placed her light jacket on her shoulders and let his hands linger an extra few seconds before saying, "Are you ready? Bye, Martha. Thanks for covering for Carol. I'll have your boss back early so she can get a good night's sleep." As they went out the door, he asked, "You wouldn't mind a picnic instead of a restaurant, would you?"

"Actually, I was so busy today, I didn't get around to making any reservations."

"I already took care of everything. I told you, you need a break. Relax." Instead of his truck, a sporty little Saturn Sky was parked in the driveway, which he explained was his Sunday fun car. They talked about the beauty of yesterday's wedding and future development of Webster House, just friendly chatter as they drove out of town through the countryside to the lake at Yellow Creek State Park.

Jonathan took a picnic basket out of the trunk, which held a red-and-white checked tablecloth, a bottle of sparkling grape juice, stemware glasses, and a gourmet picnic supper. After they ate and repacked the picnic basket, they went for a stroll on the bike path. That late on Sunday, there weren't many people around. He reached for her hand as they walked, and this time, she felt comfortable with his touch. Their quiet companionship brought her to a peace she hadn't known for quite a period of time. They watched Canada geese and a couple of Mallard ducks swimming and begging for scraps from an elderly couple.

They sat down across from each other at another picnic table where Carol was facing the lake view. Jonathan only had eyes for her. He seemed nervous but wasn't getting to any point of serious discussion until he opened the basket and served brownies for dessert and poured coffee from a thermos into two cups.

"I hope that is decaf. I am trying to reduce caffeine." She didn't offer the reason why as she added creamer from a small package and stirred it in with a plastic spoon.

He stirred his coffee even though he drank it black. He looked up from concentrating on the swirling coffee and focused on Carol. "I am trying to find...the words to tell you, ah..."

She reached over and steadied his hand before he splashed his hot coffee. His hand was warm as he held her hand softly in his work-roughened hand. The touch helped them both. "Whatever you have to say, just say it. We have been honest with each other to this point. Why stop now?"

"Carol, I want you to know how much this time with you means to me."

"This has been pleasant and relaxing. I needed this, especially today."

He looked at her and started hesitantly, "I...think...no, I know." Then he blurted out in a rush, "I love you." His eyes held hers as a silly grin spread across his tanned face. "I said it. I have been practicing for so long how to say those words. I finally said it, and I mean it. I know you are involved with Randy, yet I get vibes from you that you care for me. Before you make any plans with him, since you did catch the bouquet, well… I had to state my case. He may be the one you choose. However, before you do, please know I feel a strong connection, a bond.

"We work well together, well, not only the work part. We are good together in so many ways. I didn't mean to hit you with this all at once, but I have a feeling you are going to do something drastic with Randy. I couldn't let you do that without telling you what's in my heart. The problem is, I want more time like this with you, as much as you can give me. I feel less lost when I am with you. Although I value the friendship you offer, I want more. I want you. I know you care for Randy, but I don't believe you are really in love with him."

"I haven't made any decision to marry Randy, if that's what you are afraid of. No need to worry. I have known Randy a long time. And yes, I do love him in a way, but—"

"Carol, is it possible I am feeling you beginning to love me?"

"It's not only about love. It is the forgiveness part. Our history includes some difficult memories." She sipped her coffee to moisten her dry throat.

"But you said yourself that the past shouldn't affect our future. Don't you remember saying that? Carol, my dear one, I want you to spend the rest of your life with me. Okay, now your turn. Tell me honestly what your thoughts are." As he finished, he saw her eyes were glistening with tears on the verge of spilling over, yet she was smiling.

"Jonathan, dear Jonathan. How long have you felt this way? I have recently become aware that I have loved you for a long time. I didn't want to say anything since I didn't know how you felt. Catching the bouquet is only a tradition. And it only means that whoever catches it will be the next one to marry. Doesn't say to whom. Plus, no one is getting married anytime soon."

"Why not? Why do we have to wait? We have known each other for a year, and time moves too fast to spend a lot of time waiting to be together. Marry me, Carol, sweetheart. Let's not wait. I wanted to bring my mother's ring for you to wear, but it's her wedding band."

"If you are proposing, I want to accept. However, please let me sleep on this overnight, and I need to talk to my daughters. I am not ready to set a date until I have time to think. Randy came to see me today. And, well, I want to be the one to tell him."

Jonathan got up, walked around the picnic table, and lifted her into a hug then a lingering kiss, full of passion and promise. People seated at a nearby table, to which they had been previously oblivious, applauded and cheered.

Carol turned to the people and smiled. "Well, knowing this small town, I probably won't be the first one to break the news to Randy. You know I am struggling to put the past in the past. What will we tell people when they ask how we met?"

"We will tell them the truth. I picked you up along the highway." It made them both laugh, relieving the seriousness of the moment.

They ate their brownies, unable to stop smiling. Carol wanted to sleep on what Jonathan said but doubted there would be much sleeping again this night. She imagined not too many women received two proposals of marriage on the same day. Her head was spinning, trying to come up with the words to tell Randy and also thinking of what kind of wedding she should be planning. She already experienced an unromantic courthouse wedding. Under the rose arbor would be nice. She changed the subject, and nothing more was said about if or when they would marry. The revelation of Jonathan loving her was enough for her to think about. She was trying to get used to the idea of making even more changes to her life.

The ride home was comfortably quiet, holding hands and admiring the sun setting in the west. Jonathan walked her to her door and gave her a long tender kiss. Knowing she had something more to tell him, she added, "Could you come by tomorrow evening?"

"Sure can. I have some appointments in Lucerne. See you about six?"

After another kiss goodbye, Carol reached for the door, waving at Jonathan as he got into his sports car. She stood for a moment alone on the porch, trying to get her emotions under control. She wasn't ready to share this with anyone yet.

Martha, holding Penny the cat while sitting on the sofa, saw a different look on Carol's face when she entered the living room to say good night. From her expression, she knew without being told. "I knew it, Carol. I'm so happy for you. Now do you want to talk?" She had seen the love growing between Carol and Jonathan over the months he built Jim and Melissa's house. They had a girl-to-girl talk that lasted past midnight before going to their rooms.

Knowing Randy liked to run before going to his office, Carol set her alarm for six thirty. She needed to talk with him. Alone in her room at last, Carol could sort out her jumbled thoughts. As she prepared for bed, she remembered a talk she had with her mother a long time ago about all the different kinds of love. Ma's words came back to her. *"A person can love parents, brothers, aunts, uncles, grandparents, teachers, and friends. Each love is different from that one special love you will find someday. That special love will be deeper and stronger than all others. A simple touch will make your fingers tingle with excitement. A smile will reach into your heart. A shared look will make you feel you two are alone, even in a crowded room. When that kind of love comes along, you will know."* Ma had wisely described her feelings about Jonathan. Finally, thinking of Ma's words, she slept.

She awoke knowing she could make the right decision. Her mind was clear on who deserved her love in that special way. She couldn't marry Randy; it didn't work before because their form of love wasn't strong enough. The passing years hadn't changed that. To her reflection in the bathroom mirror, she said, "He is more like a brother to me. We have a special friendship—that's all, not enough to build a life on." She had her answer; her decision was clear. She donned jeans, a T-shirt, light sweater, and running shoes, and met Randy as he was stretching out at the bench in the park. "Good morning, Randy. Mind if I run with you? We need to talk."

"Yeah, I know already," he grumbled so quietly she barely heard him.

"How could you know what I want to say?"

"I got the news late last night from my cousin and two clients. They wanted to ask how I was under the circumstances. I asked them, 'What circumstances do you mean?' My cousin said he thought you were my girl. However, you were at Yellow Creek Park being overly friendly with the contractor he met Saturday at Jim and Melissa's wedding reception. My clients said basically the same thing." Randy was avoiding Carol's eyes as he spoke. "I got the message loud and clear, although it wasn't much of a surprise. I saw it coming, and I did nothing to prevent it. I learned a long time ago I couldn't win every case. The evidence was clearly not on my side."

"There wasn't anything you could do. If you are really, truly, my friend, you could be happy for me. I have been alone and independent too long while deliberately avoiding getting involved with any man while raising my girls. They are barely out of the nest, and I see there is a whole lot of life left to live. Yes, I still love you, Randy. That won't change. However, I realize I'm not *in* love with you. There is a difference. Marrying you would be a mistake. In my estimation, I would be going backward. I am also remembering why it didn't work for us before. You have to admit there is something lacking in our relationship. Do you feel excited to see me or just a comfortable feeling when we are together? Jonathan makes me feel young, beautiful, desired. No, it's not about sex. We are attracted like two magnets. Oh well. I guess I am having trouble finding adequate words to explain my feelings."

"Oh I understand, Carol. More than you know. You are right. You and I are comfortable together. I thought you felt as I do—a good friendship is a strong basis for a marriage, a partnership of sorts. However, you seem to have found that special, elusive love. I see it in your eyes. I am happy for you. I have had all night to think about this. You're doing the right thing. Best wishes to you in your new life. Just don't wait. Grab the brass ring while you can." He gave her a lopsided smile followed by a brotherly hug and kiss on the forehead. "You don't need to run with me. There is nothing more to say on the subject."

"I'm sorry, Randy."

"Don't be. Now go. Make plans for a good life ahead." When he looked up the path leading around the lake, he saw a familiar figure dressed in her Kelly-green running outfit coming toward him. He realized he was looking forward to running with his faithful secretary Mamie this morning. It wasn't a coincidence they kept meeting this way. Since she knew his schedule, he realized she was also enjoying their time together away from the office as they had been running together several times a week over the last few months. He was happy to see her smiling face and bouncing red hair. "Wait up, Mamie. I'll be with you in a minute."

Turning back to Carol, he added, "Your brother Jim made a correct statement the day your mother's will was read when he said, 'There are none so blind as those who won't see.' I have had something, no, *someone* right in front of me all these years. I *do* understand what you said about being comfortable versus a special spark. I think we are both lucky to have discovered that before we made a mistake. I will always be your friend, Carol. But I see we both need to avail ourselves of other options." He waved to Carol over his shoulder and ran to catch up with Mamie as she was running in place while waiting for him. They disappeared over the small hill on the way around lake, running side by side on the narrow path.

Carol was glad he understood. She knew Randy would follow his own destiny as she had discovered hers. She was home. Who said you can't go home again?

50

AN UNDERSTANDING

Jonathan arrived early on Monday evening after his last appointment with a local shop renter wanting to build a house. After supper, Tony took Martha on a movie date. Once settled on the back porch with their glasses of lemonade, Carol continued their conversation from the day before.

"I have given your proposal serious thought. How could I not love you? You bring excitement into my life. I too feel less lost when you are near. You make me happy to be alive. I have a lot to tell you, but that can wait. For now, let me give you an answer. I realize I want you too. I have thought long and hard over the last twenty-four hours. I am ready, as of this minute, to put the past in the past and offer you more than friendship. My answer is yes. I will marry you. Would you be able to move to Lucerne? I can't leave my newfound joy in running Webster House."

Jonathan took Carol into his arms and sealed their joy with a kiss. "I have been hoping all night and all day that you could find enough love in your heart to say that. And yes, I can and will move to Lucerne. I received many job opportunities in and around Lucerne over my work on your B&B and Jim and Melissa's house. In fact, I may be moving here even if you weren't willing to forgive and forget."

They leaned on each other while watching the sun setting behind the grapevines on the hill as she told him the whole story about her dad's illness, Ma's will, the background of her mother's restoration of Lucerne, and her shock over the inheritance left to her and her brothers.

Jonathan grew excited while listening then revealed he wasn't just a carpenter. "My father was a miner too. He died in a cave-in when Jacob and I were only five. My mother moved us in with her parents when she went to work to support us. Our grandparents raised us while Mom worked. The coal company eventually settled the wrongful-death suit, and the payoff has been growing in investments. I have inherited means of my own and would be thrilled to join you in an effort to bring new life to a town suffering from the effects of the mining industry.

"I did know of the change in Lucerne. I had no idea who was behind the new growth. When I left my wife, Jacob invited me to live with him, and we started the Virginia service station. I went to Williamstown to help my Uncle Merle in the construction company when he got sick, and he left that company to me." They went into the kitchen to have a piece of leftover wedding cake and discuss plans for their rosy future.

By the time Jonathan left for home, they had a plan for a local office in what used to be Jim's back garage. He would have a new local phone number and spend time developing a local clientele and move from Williamstown as soon as all those projects around there are completed. His workers lived halfway in between, so it would not be a problem for them.

Jonathan would live in whatever building they were restoring until their wedding, and then move into Webster House with Carol after they were married. They were looking toward to starting a new life for both of them, each looking ahead to a bright future.

PART 4

SUMMER THROUGH FALL 2016

51

SURPRISE IN STORE

Michaela Joy Watson, at eighteen, a recent high school graduate, was taking the summer off before attending Penn State to become a veterinarian. A few months ago, she did a DNA test just out of curiosity. The results she received in the mail a month ago indicated she could be related to a list of relatives she already knew on her mother's side.

The father she had known her whole life was not listed as a possible relative nor was anyone else on his side that she considered family. Instead, there was a Jonathan Michael Harrison listed whose last known address was Williamstown, Pennsylvania; a Jacob Dean Harrison from Tyson Corner, Virginia; Olive Reagan and Elizabeth Johnson both from Holidaysburg, Pennsylvania; and more Harrisons, now deceased.

When she told her grandmother Hudson about this puzzling revelation, Grammie was the one to reveal, while on her sickbed, that Michaela's biological father was most likely Jonathan Harrison. "Your mother was married to Jonathan Harrison for a short time, and he was responsible for someone dying. He shot someone, supposedly accidentally, and was cleared by the police department and courts. He left town soon after.

"Your mother divorced him, claiming she was abandoned. She must have been pregnant when he moved away to start a business with his brother in Virginia, and she never made any attempt to contact him after papers were signed and the divorce decree issued.

Your mother quickly married her former boyfriend, and no questions were asked."

How could he be as nice as her grammie said he was? No one had seen him for more than eighteen years; he could be someone totally different. Grammie didn't live long enough to give her any more details. Michaela learned only part of the truth and realized her mother lied to her for her whole life.

She took the results to her mother and shared the report without revealing what her grandmother told her. "Mother, my DNA results say I might be related to Jonathan and Jacob Harrison and a whole list of Harrisons, Olive Reagan, and Elizabeth Johnson. I have never met anyone by those names at family reunions. Do those names mean anything to you? Do you know who they are?"

"Well yes, I do, Mickey. Jonathan Harrison and I were married for only a short time. He was—okay *is*—your biological father. He never knew about you. I divorced him when he left town after a scandal about someone dying. The investigation cleared him, but he couldn't or wouldn't forgive me for my part in the situation. I took back my maiden name and then married Charles Watson. This is old history. It shouldn't matter now! You were raised by two loving parents."

"Why have you lied to me all these years? I grew up thinking my dad was my biological father. All this time, my real father was out there? Why didn't he even know about me? I want the truth, and I want it now!"

"Okay, Michaela. You want the truth? I'll give you the truth. I suppose you are old enough now to understand. Just sit down and stop pacing. You make me nervous. As I said, Jonathan Harrison is your biological father. Jacob is his twin brother. Your dad, Charles Watson, loved you until the day he died. He was there for you, unlike Jonathan who abandoned me. Not that I blame him.

"To be honest, Jonathan is a wonderful, kind, sweet-natured man, at least he was all those years ago. I was a wild child. After all the wedding excitement was over and reality set in, I didn't like being married. I still wanted to do other things than being a stay-at-home wife. I worked a few days a week at the local company store for some spending money. Jonathan worked at Stephenson Lumber and did carpentry work on weekends. His Uncle Merle taught him carpentry while he lived with his grandparents after his father died in a mining accident.

"Jonathan liked to go hunting, and I hated him for killing defenseless animals. I have always loved animals, just like you do. He brought home his dead game and expected me to cook it. I wanted to go out partying, dancing, and do fun stuff. He was always working or hunting.

"Through my job, I met this sweet-talking salesman who told me he would take me away from housewife drudgery. He said he was going to go home and tell his dowdy wife he wanted a divorce. He was looking for excitement too. He planned to stay in town overnight since the weather was stormy. Since my husband was hunting in the mountains, I invited Ted to spend the night with me."

Michaela jumped up from her chair and resumed pacing. "Mother, how could you? You were married to a nice guy and you invited another man, a *stranger*, into your home?" Michaela was getting red in the face from the anger she was feeling toward her mother's irresponsible behavior.

"Listen to me, Michaela, and sit down. He wasn't a stranger. We had been talking at the store for months. I planned to tell Jonny when he got home that I wanted a divorce so I would be free to marry Ted. I was young. I was foolish. I was lonely, okay? How was I to know Jonathan would come home early? The weather was bad for him up in the mountains too, and it looked as though it would not clear out for a few days.

"We heard a heavy vehicle's tires crunch on the gravel driveway. I peeked through the bedroom curtains and saw Jonny's pickup. Ted grabbed his clothes and went out the second-story window to climb down the lattice enclosing the porch. Jonny's headlights shone on Ted during his descent, and he raised the gun he was carrying and fired a warning shot. The shot must have ricocheted off a tree, hitting Ted, who fell onto our concrete patio and died. The coroner determined the minor gunshot wound didn't kill him. His fall onto the concrete did. Jonny explained to the police he thought Ted was climbing up to break into the bedroom where my lights were on. He was protecting me.

"There was an investigation revealing Ted was just an opportunist. He told other women the same story in several more towns along Route 422. Four other young women came forward claiming they were engaged to Ted when his death was announced on the news. Since Jonny voluntarily told his story, the investigation was over quickly. He was cleared of any wrongdoing due to all the character witnesses who told police what a nice guy he was: churchgoer, do-goody, and up-standing citizen with an unfaithful wife. He was considered a victim and left town immediately after being cleared. I divorced him on abandonment, broke the lease on the rental house, and moved to Cresson to be closer to my parents.

"By then, I suspected I was expecting. It turns out I was just barely pregnant on that awful night Teddy died. I reconnected with and quickly married my high school sweetheart Charles, the man who raised you as his own child even though I was slightly pregnant when we married. There is no doubt who your father is. You have Jonny's curly brown hair, blue eyes, and those dimples. You are Jonny's girl all right.

"Charles insisted I have a paternity test done using hair from a hairbrush Jonny left behind. I had a box full of some of his belongings to give him if I ever saw him again. But he never came back. Or if he did, I was already living here in Cresson. I kept the paternity report in case this matter came up someday.

"I guess I can't blame you if you want to find him. I have no idea where he is living. Last I knew, he had some aunts still living in Holidaysburg. You can do an internet search. You have my blessing. However, don't tell him I said hello. He hates me, and to tell the truth, I can't blame him. You probably do too." She was blubbering into a handkerchief by the time she finished talking.

"No, Mother, I don't hate you. However, I am on the fence about forgiving you. I understand you were young, foolish, lonely, and may I add *stupid* to that list? One thing I have learned is, we must take responsibility for our actions. Lying only complicates the issue. Thanks for the good upbringing you and *Charles* gave me. But

I am going to find my real father. Thanks for the graduation gift of the truth. I'll keep in touch, but I am going to find my real father and discover who I really am!"

The internet search revealed there was a Jonathan M. Harrison, owner of Harrison Construction in Williamstown, Pennsylvania. On the Contact Us information, she got an address, phone number, and hours of operation. *Won't he be surprised when I show up?* She checked a map for the location of Williamstown.

She called the phone number after business hours and listened to a recorded message. She really didn't want to make this announcement over the phone. They would be face to face when he got this news. A female voice gave a recorded message, saying, "Thank you for calling Harrison Construction Company. Mr. Harrison is opening another office in Lucerne, PA. You may leave a message and he will get back to you, or call 724-555-WORK. That is 724-555-9675. Have a great day."

She located Lucerne on the map. That was a bit closer than Williamstown. She spent a few days, with her mother helping, gathering documentation for proof of who she was. Like it or not, Jonathan Harrison had a surprise coming. She packed a small bag, put all her documentation in a graduation gift briefcase, and took off on a journey that would change her life—for better or worse remained to be seen.

52

REACHING OUT

While driving her VW Bug, Michaela kept asking herself, *What is my alleged father going to say?* Long light-brown curly hair would be blowing in her face if not for her ponytail captured in her hat. She decided to stop at Lucerne and check things out since it was on the way to Williamstown where she would look for the office for Harrison Construction Company.

She was still adjusting to the fact that the man she thought was her father wasn't. When Michaela was old enough to realize her parents' anniversary and her birthday didn't make sense, her mother said, "Well, some babies are just born early." She never knew her mother was first married to someone other than the man she thought was her father.

Michaela turned left off Route 119 onto Lucerne Road at the traffic light. Entering Lucerne at the west end, she drove by several farms, a B&B named Webster House, several churches, and then entered the business district. She was still asking herself how to make her introduction. *Hello, Father. I am Michaela, the daughter you don't know exists.* Or should she act cool, get to know the guy first? Who knows what kind of person he is after all these years.

She drove the length of Lucerne's Main Street, noting the clean appearance of businesses with freshly painted signs. She parked her VW Bug next to the small duck pond and Town Park and wandered in and out of some of the shops, bought some flowers at Bloomers, and browsed The Company Store out of curiosity.

Nearing lunchtime, she entered Sweet Stuff Shop and purchased a cinnamon roll and a cup of tea and sat at a café table next to the window to watch people walking by. Everyone seemed friendly, stopping to chat with each other as they passed by. As each man passed the window, she thought, *He could be my father*. She made up stories about each one until her head was spinning with her confusion and frustration.

She was still sitting there when the guy she saw at The Company Store came in. "Hi, Daisy. I need a dozen of doughnuts. Family business meetin' this weekend. Rob is comin' home too. Carol and Jonathan have some expansion idea they want to propose. I can't wait to hear. Give me an assortment. Rob will eat most of them anyway. Carol is determined to keep her girlish figure. Jonathan burns off his calories with hard work."

Of course, Michaela's ears perked up hearing the name Jonathan. That was her first inclination her father might actually live here.

"Sure, Jim. Haven't seen you since your honeymoon. How is the lucky lady?"

"She is every man's dream come true. Thanks for askin'."

"Glad to fix you up with the doughnuts. I'll throw in a cinnamon roll too since I know Jonathan buys one when he comes in." Daisy continued her friendly patter, exchanging small talk about the weather and what a wonderful summer day it was. This was certainly service with a smile while she carefully packaged his doughnuts and cinnamon roll. Jim included Michaela with a friendly smile as he walked out the door.

Was her taste for cinnamon rolls inherited from her father? "Hi again," she said as she approached Daisy. "Could you tell me where there is a good place to stay in town? Doesn't have to be fancy."

"Well, there are motels out on the four lane, but if you want to experience the essence of Lucerne, go west to Webster House B&B located at the edge of town. It's a family-run business. The Websters are really nice folks. That was Jim Webster who just left. His sister Carol and her brothers, and now joined by her fiancé Jonathan

Harrison, are reviving this old town. It used to be a dirty, rundown coal-mining town. They are renovating, building, and making this into a resort town. There is so much to do around here. Hope you plan to stay awhile."

She swallowed the lump in her throat for having found Jonathan Harrison so easily. "Thanks. I think I'll go check it out. I am taking my time to look for a good summer job. I just graduated from high school. I can go back to volunteer at the Cresson Veterinary Clinic where I worked the last two summers, but I am also available for a new adventure if it comes my way. I am staying open. You never know what might develop."

Michaela smiled and left, cheered by the soft chiming of the bell above the door. There was something about the people in this town. She was usually rather reserved around strangers and didn't understand why she shared so much with Daisy.

Michaela got back into her car, did a U-turn, and found Webster House B&B's entrance. When she got out of the car, she took a deep breath of newly mown hay in the air, enjoying peaceful surroundings. She liked being in the country atmosphere yet close to town. The buildings and lawn were well kept with an inviting swing and some comfortable-looking rocking chairs on the porch. She was tempted to sit down and relax. However, she first needed to check if there were any rooms available. There were other cars in the parking area. Perhaps they were full.

Just then, a sleek black Mercedes pulled into the lot. She didn't want the Mercedes driver to get the last available room if that were the case. She quickly rang the doorbell and then entered through the screen door when a pleasant female voice called out, "Come on in. We are open." The Mercedes driver followed her in, without hesitating or ringing the bell, acting as though he owned the place.

A female who must have announced, "We are open," rose from a small desk in the foyer. She greeted Michaela with a friendly smile and said, "I'll be right with you, but first…" She gave the guy who entered behind Michaela a big hug and an affectionate pat on his three-day beard. Then, she turned and addressed Michaela. "What can I do for you now that I have properly welcomed my brother Rob? I am Carol Webster, part owner of Webster House."

Michaela was slightly confused. If the guy named Jim who bought the doughnuts was this guy's brother, they didn't look much alike. But Carol was a little bit like both of them. This must be the Carol who was engaged to the man named Jonathan Harrison. "Hello, I am Michaela Watson. I was wondering if you have a room available? I am in the area on personal business, and I have no idea how long I will be staying. A simple room for one would be good, nothing fancy."

Although she was living on a small inheritance her Grammie Hudson left her, she didn't know how long it would take her to actually find and introduce herself to her father; plus, she still had college tuition to pay. No use squandering her limited funds. She was still angry with her mother and would not be asking for a dime from her. She needed a job as soon as she resolved her father issue. Applications for student loans would be necessary.

"Yes, we have several rooms available. We have one I favor with a view to the hills behind the house. That would place you away from the family rooms. We are having a meeting this weekend. I hope we won't be too noisy for you. Just tell us to tone it down if we get rowdy. Feel free to enjoy the TV in the living room. We don't have TVs in guest rooms to encourage a more family-like atmosphere. Plus, the sound travels in these old houses. Just fill out this register, and I will see you to your room in a minute.

"Breakfasts and dinners are included. People are usually out and about during the day. But if you are here, you can share a sandwich with Martha or me, whoever is here. Rob, be a dear and help Miss Watson get her bag from her car and take it on up to the Oak View room. Miss Watson, dinner will be served at 5:45 tonight as soon as everyone gathers. If you want privacy, you may take a tray to your room, but we would be pleased to have you join with the family."

Michaela filled out the register and handed Carol her credit card for processing. With paperwork completed, Rob helped her with her small bag, although she could have managed on her own. From the front seat, she gathered her bouquet of flowers and the briefcase containing information she collected before starting her trip to find her father. Rob gave her a running dialogue about the history of the B&B, and she found out he was an airline pilot and traveled the world. He kept talking and never asked why she was in town, for which she felt grateful.

When Carol saw her carrying a small bouquet of flowers, a vase filled with water magically appeared. "Thank you, Ms. Webster. You are so kind. Please call me Michaela. Miss Watson sounds too formal." Michaela was impressed with how friendly Carol was. There was a kindness in her eyes; and to think, this could soon be my father's wife, my stepmother. *We'll see how kind she is when she finds out who I am!*

"Then you call me Carol. We don't stand on ceremony here."

She followed Rob up the stairs, admiring the woodwork and cleanliness. Alone in her comfortable room, she opened her briefcase and once more looked over her papers she kept in a red file folder. She spread everything out on the bed: her mother's paternity report, her DNA report, her birth certificate listing Charles Watson as her father, a copy of her mother and Jonathan's marriage license and divorce decree, pictures of her mother she took from one of the photo albums, a selection of pictures of herself as a child.

Unfortunately, photos from her mother's first marriage were either destroyed or lost during her move. To top it off, she brought with her the contents from the box of Jonathan's belongings her mother kept all those years. She wondered if she would need all these items to prove to Jonathan Harrison who she was. She rehearsed her introduction once more. *Hello. I am the child you abandoned.* What would he do? What would he say? Would he throw her out of the house? Carol was so friendly and welcoming. How would Carol react? What would she say?

Then, her thoughts turned again. *What if the report is wrong? Maybe this was all a big mistake. How foolish will I feel if this man is not my biological father? Was Mother still lying to me?* Michaela felt totally betrayed and unsure of herself. *Why couldn't I have left well enough alone?* She did not unpack her bag and had half a notion to go back downstairs and tell Carol she changed her mind about staying.

She gathered up her papers and put them safely back into her briefcase, put her small suitcase next to the door, and then glanced out the window at the lovely scenery. Oak View was an appropriate name for this room. There was a great red oak tree in the back yard, a rose arbor, and flower gardens. She watched a calico cat cross the yard. In a neighboring field, two horses were grazing on the greenest grass she had seen in a long time.

She sat down in a cozy rocking chair, and the movement and view calmed her. *Okay, girl. Time to get real. I will spend the night, meet this guy Jonathan Harrison, and not say a word about any of this until…until when? When is the right time to make this life-changing announcement to a strange man?*

After a short rest, Michaela went back downstairs. Carol invited her to have a toasted cheese sandwich, and they shared some small talk. Carol added to Rob's rundown of the history of Webster House and the town. Michaela was shown the in-house library where she picked out a book for later in the evening. She decided to take a walk around town. Perhaps she would run into Jonathan Harrison.

She didn't find her alleged father, but she did get a good look at the surroundings. *Peaceful* was the one word she could come up with as a description. She sat down on the bench at the duck pond. She did relent and called her mother to tell her where she was, the trip was uneventful, and she already had a lead on where Jonathan Harrison might be. "Yes, Mother, I know this is going to be a shock to him. I know my manners. Yes, Mother, I will be cautious. Yes, Mother, I'll let you know when, or if, I find him."

She walked back to Webster House and sat on the porch in a rocking chair watching cars driving by and the cows in a distant pasture. The calico cat found her, jumped in her lap, and promptly set to purring her pleasure at having someone pet her. Feeling drowsy from her early morning drive, she went back upstairs to her room with the cat following her. She tried to read her book; but the bed was so comfortable, she woke up much later with a start, realizing it was nearly suppertime. She needed to change from her traveling clothes.

53

A NEW FAMILY

At 5:40 p.m., Michaela was changed from her traveling outfit of jeans and tee to dress in a blue-flowered sundress that brought out the blue in her eyes. She combed out her wind-tangled, sleep-flattened hair, letting curls loosely frame her lovely face although a glance in the mirror reminded her of her anger toward her mother. She might have her biological father's eye and hair color and dimples, but the shape of her eyes and mouth looked like her mother.

She walked downstairs quietly, not wanting to disrupt the active family discussion going on in the kitchen. She walked to the kitchen doorway to ask, "Is there anything I can do to help?" Carol Webster was in the kitchen with three men. One she recognized as Jim from The Company Store who was talking to Rob, the pilot and Mercedes guy whom she met earlier. The other man was standing with his back to her, tossing a salad and talking to Carol. She could see his curly brown hair. He was tall, thin, and soft-spoken. Her heart began to race.

Carol heard the offer to help and said, while turning to greet her, "There you are. We thought you might have fallen asleep. Guys, quiet down. I want you to meet Michaela Watson, our guest for at least this evening. Michaela, you met Rob earlier. That handsome dude is my brother, Jim Webster. His wife, Melissa, is the one setting the dining room table."

"Hello, Michaela," came softly from the dining room.

Gently laying her hand on the other man's arm, Carol proudly continued the introductions, "Last but not least, this handsome guy is my fiancé, Jonathan Harrison."

Jonathan turned to greet their newest guest, and he stared at her as much as she was staring at him. When her mother told Michaela there was no doubt Jonathan was her father, she totally understood when he was there in front of her: same hair, same eye color, and she could see if he smiled, there would be dimples, like hers.

No one spoke. No one moved except Jim who said, "Hi, Michaela Watson. I saw you earlier at Sweet Stuff. Make yourself at home. Enjoy your stay."

However, Michaela couldn't find her voice to respond. Gradually, Jonathan gained his composure and walked toward her, starting to offer his hand. "Have we met, Miss Watson? You look like someone I knew a long time ago."

"No, we have never met, but you might have known my mother, Grace. Hudson was her maiden name." Her rehearsed speech was totally forgotten in her shock of meeting face to face the man who, obviously, gave her life.

Jonathan stopped in midstep and brought his outstretched hand up to run through his hair. "You are Grace's daughter?" he said with total disbelief. Still not breaking eye contact with her, Jonathan stepped forward to gently take her hand in his.

"Yes, that's what I said. Grace Hudson is my mother. I just graduated from high school and am in the area on personal business, looking for a summer job. Daisy at Sweet Stuff told me this is a good place to stay while in town for a few days…on personal business." She was repeating herself in her stunned lack of composure. She could see Jonathan was mentally doing some calculations.

All of a sudden, he let go of her hand and said, "We are ready for supper. Why don't you sit next to me and tell me all about yourself? We are happy to have you join us for however long you can stay." He quickly gathered up the salad bowl and tongs to head for the dining room.

Carol was looking back and forth between Jonathan and Michaela. Although she didn't see it before, she did see the resemblance now with them standing next to each other with her curly brown hair falling loosely over her shoulders, and the shining bright-blue eyes. There would be some explaining done before the evening was over. She didn't know he was keeping secrets, and this secret was monumental.

The kitchen became active again as they all picked up food dishes and trouped into the dining room, chairs scraping on the old plank floor. Rob said a blessing, and everyone picked up bowls and started passing them around the great old oak dining table. Throughout supper, Jonathan kept up a running conversation with easy, however revealing, questions. He seemed very interested when she revealed she wanted to be a veterinarian. By the time dessert was served, table cleared, and everyone headed to the back porch to enjoy fireflies dancing over the lawn, she knew she did not need to make any prepared speech. She tried to excuse herself, but Jonathan took her elbow and led her out with the family.

They spread out to sit in rockers or the porch swing. Jonathan leaned over to Michaela, "Would you like to see more of the property before it is totally dark?" They were barely out of earshot of the others when he asked, "When is your birthday?"

"I was eighteen on May 30." Michaela again watched him do the mental math.

He turned and looked at her again. "I had no idea. I didn't object to your mother getting a divorce. I quickly signed the papers I was served. If I had known about you, I wouldn't have been absent in your life. Please believe me. I don't know how much she told you. If you have questions, I would be pleased to fill in any details, painful as it might be. And I am curious about what your middle name is."

"My middle name is Joy." She saw his accepting reaction. "Oh, I believe you. She explained everything to me, if I can believe what she said after lying to me my whole life. I don't want to cause you any problems. I only wanted to meet you. Now that I have, I'll be on my way. Really, I don't want anything. I was curious. You have a good life here from what I can tell. Don't give me a second thought. My mother married a good man, and I was raised as his daughter. He died of cancer last year, but I had a good life. I didn't know anything about any of this until a short time ago really." She explained the sequence of events, and he was amazed at how this revelation came about.

"No way, young lady. I am sorry about your grandmother Hudson. She was always nice to me. But now I know you exist. I want to get to know you, everything about you. What you eat, what kind of music you like. You must like horses and other animals based on your career choice. Please stay until we become friends, at the very least. Penny has certainly accepted you as part of the family. Did your mother tell you why she chose Joy for your middle name?"

"No. I don't even know anyone by that name."

"That was my mother's name, and my middle name is Michael. She had to have known I was your father from the beginning. That was nice of her to give you names from my side of the family. Next time you speak to her, let her know that I understand the events of the past and it's time to finally put everything to rest."

"I will do that. She thinks you hate her. I think she still feels guilty, as well she should. As far as getting to know each other, I found out one thing today. We both prefer cinnamon rolls to doughnuts."

At that statement, Jonathan gave her a dimple-revealing smile and laughed out loud, reaching out for her and giving her a fatherly hug. They admired the sleek brown horses and Penny the cat as she followed them on their walk. As they approached the porch, Carol joined them near the memorial garden. "Jonathan, is there something you wish to share with me?" Carol asked with a big smile lighting up her face.

"Carol, this is my daughter, Michaela Joy Watson. I swear I knew nothing about her existence—until today. But now that I do, I want to include her in our business venture. Don't we need a veterinarian in Lucerne? I want to see what we can do about keeping her near. I love your daughters, but I never imagined having my own daughter one day. I missed the diapers and drool stages, but let's recapture what we can."

"Yes. Welcome, Michaela. I figured it out when I saw you together. Thank you for finding Jonathan and me. I have a daughter near your age studying to be a veterinarian technician. We'd be pleased and proud to share our humble home with you. Please think about staying. For now, take time to acquaint yourself with your father. He's a special person."

Michaela welcomed the embrace from Carol as tears welled up in her eyes. "I could stay awhile, but only if you let me help in some way."

"Don't worry about that," Jonathan assured her. "Running a B&B is a 24-7 job. Stick around and find out."

"I am going to college in September. But I'll think about spending the summer. This is all too much to absorb in such a short time."

"Well, as your father, I will certainly help with your college expenses and try to make up for time we have lost. I hope you are going to a school close enough for frequent visits. Now that I know you exist, I don't want to lose touch."

"Is Penn State close enough? Also, people who are close to me call me Mickey."

54

LIFE GOES ON

Jonathan and Carol made plans to marry after the busy tourist season was over, which gave them several months to make plans. For the time being, they were happy just being together when possible while leading busy lives.

They treasured their late Sunday afternoons and evenings when they drove back to Yellow Creek Park, walked the bike trail, and spent time sharing memories of their growing-up years, getting more background on which to build their relationship rather than concentrating on painful memories.

Meanwhile, Mickey was getting to know her father, working at a job at a veterinary clinic in a neighboring town. They spent Saturdays together. She insisted on paying rent for one of Carol's furnished apartments, then drove home to Cresson to retrieve some more of her belongings. She explained the arrangement to her mother, who gave her a hug and said, "I am happy for you. Jonathan is a decent man. I have many regrets in life. I should have treated him better. I just wasn't grown up enough at the time." Forgiveness was possible.

Mickey also helped Carol do cleanup after guests left Sunday mornings on busy weekends, getting to know her as a generous, forgiving, and loving person. Before long, Mickey and Susie, at home from school for the summer, were interacting as sisters.

Jonathan was traveling back and forth from Williamstown and Lucerne before finally moving into an upstairs apartment in one of the buildings they purchased and were restoring. He did some more work on the back garage to create an attractive office setting rather than try to operate a second business out of the B&B.

Jim and Melissa were happily purchasing additional decorations for their new home. They added a gazebo in the backyard equipped with a swing and other creature comforts one forgets to do when building a new home.

Jim reported seeing Randy and Mamie having lunch together at the deli on weekends while home from Harrisburg. They were seen together at various social events, plus running together at the lake. Martha reported seeing them at the movie together. It was nearly impossible to keep secrets in this small community.

As for Martha and Tony, they were getting closer and hinted there would be another wedding sometime in the future. Martha's sisters, Hannah and Lucy, came from Lancaster to visit her and approved of Tony and her new lifestyle. She was happy to have at least part of her family in touch once more. The last year had been a total change for her, and she was enjoying every minute.

Time was moving quickly as summer turned to fall. The display of colored leaves brought more visitors to the area. Carol was appreciating all the extra help until Susie and Mickey went to school in mid-September. She was overjoyed at the friendship they had developed due to their common interests. They were already planning their partnership and scouting for the perfect spot for their new clinic after graduation.

Jonathan was proving to be a great dad and was looking forward to becoming Susan's stepdad after the upcoming wedding.

55

LOVE IN THE AIR

Am I doing the right thing? Carol asked her reflection in the dressing table mirror as she applied a touch of makeup on the one-year anniversary of Webster House's opening weekend. *Has it only been a little more than a year ago since I made my life-changing move back to Pennsylvania? Everything that happened in the past fifteen months is difficult to absorb.*

As though there were an angel sitting on top of the mirror, she received an affirmation she was, indeed, doing the right thing. *It is time to put aside even an iota of doubt and start another new phase of life. The feelings of love for Jonathan are real."* She nodded and smiled to the reflection of a happy woman's reflection. She and Jonathan would work as hard on their future as they did in restoring the old farmhouse to be a successful B&B and continue renovating various properties around town.

To ease the B&B's workload and to accommodate the large turnout expected for their wedding, they decided to have their ceremony at Fellowship Presbyterian Church and their reception in the church's social room. She turned over running Webster House to Martha and all the volunteers who came forth for this one special day. She had no reason to worry about anything today except getting to the church on time.

Susan, Michaela, and Roberta, with her fiancé Duane Montgomery, arrived yesterday afternoon and were finished serving lunch to family members in the kitchen. Jonathan spent the last few nights at his place in Williamstown getting the house ready to rent to his foreman, who would continue construction projects for that area.

With her touch of makeup skillfully applied, Carol carefully slid her wedding outfit over her head, careful to not muss the upsweep Heidi created earlier that morning. Rather than wearing white, she chose a dress in pale-blue silk, midcalf length, with a brocade jacket since the weather had already turned cool. The coordinated hat had a tiny fluff of netting to represent a veil, but she realized she was long past that tradition. She slipped into her modest pumps and placed her good luck pieces in her small handbag.

For something borrowed, she wore a pearl ring of next-door neighbor Nora's that matched her mother's pearl necklace. Something blue was her dress and a small hankie hand croqueted by Grandmother Webster, which was also something old. She also carried a small New Testament given to her by Grammie Smith on her tenth birthday. Teardrop pearl earrings fulfilled something new, a wedding gift from Jonathan, given to her last evening after the rehearsal at the church and dinner at The Point.

Jacob Harrison hosted when the two families came together and had a good, get-acquainted social affair. Jonathan's two elderly aunts came all the way from Holidaysburg to join in the fun. They were sure surprised to meet Michaela but certainly acknowledged she looked so much like her father, there could be no doubt. Jacob also met his niece the day before. He was quite taken with her intelligence and passion for animals. She would make a great veterinarian.

Finally, dressed for the wedding ceremony, she went downstairs to greet family members. Everyone was there. Rob brought Heidi to Carol's great satisfaction. She could imagine a future together for those two. Jim and Melissa walked across the field from their home to join in the preparations. With her daughters and Jonathan's daughter Michaela, smiling and applauding her entrance, Carol was already fighting back tears. She performed a slight curtsy and announced, "I'm ready. Let's go do this." She picked up her bouquet of carnations interspersed with late-blooming roses from the garden.

Rob and Heidi drove her to the church in his Mercedes. She and her attendants slipped into a Sunday school room to await a signal from Heidi when the men were in place, and she and her daughters would walk down the aisle when the organist started the "Wedding March." She would do this walk on her own. She was giving herself fully to Jonathan.

56

A NEW BEGINNING

Jonathan and his brother Jacob arrived at the church in plenty of time. This was the best day of Jonathan's life as far as he was concerned. On the way to the church, Jonathan admitted to Jacob, "I never thought I would find love again after the disaster of my first marriage. No, it wasn't a disaster. Out of that union, I was given a daughter, one I have grown to love and cherish."

Jacob was positioned as a lookout to watch for Carol's arrival while Jonathan went over the final arrangements at the church. He made sure the flowers and candles were in place. He went to the social room to check on the servers, table setups, and a special cake they designed together. When he was finished checking all the details, he went into the narthex to wait. Although not superstitious, he felt there was no good tempting fate by seeing the bride before the ceremony. Jacob came to let him know a black Mercedes had parked at the front door, and Rob Webster was opening the back door for a beautiful lady all dressed in blue silk.

"That's my lady, Jacob. She knows how much I like her to wear blue to bring out the brilliance of her eyes," Jonathan said with obvious pride in his voice. "Now you are sure you have Mother's ring?"

"Yes, Jon," he said. "For the fifth time, yes. And I won't drop it, I promise."

Jacob peeked through a slit of opened door to report the church was nearly full. "There are quite a few on the groom side. I do see

Michaela sitting in the front row with aunts Olive and Elizabeth. The others must be clients or friends you made through the men's choir you joined."

"I have made friends in the town, you know? I wasn't sure if Mickey would decide to sit on the groom's side of the church or sit with Susan since they have become such good friends after getting acquainted. They are in a lot of the same classes. Their clinic will make a great addition to this town when they finish at Penn State. Man, I can hardly wait."

Jacob teased him a bit. "For today or for the vet office?"

"Both." Jonathan looked as happy as Jacob had ever seen him. Both dimples were in full display. The Harrison twins were ready. Jacob was looking forward to spending more time with the organist during the reception.

The pastor came in and told them it was time for them to take their position by the chancel steps. As they followed the pastor into the sanctuary, Jonathan saw Randy and Mamie sitting near the front, looking quite cozy together. Carol's brothers were grinning at him. Rob gave him two thumbs-up; Jim gave him a salute. Roberta and Susan both blew him air kisses as they proceeded down the aisle before Carol's entrance. He was going to be welcomed into this family without any problem. He would do his best, as he promised them last night at the rehearsal, to treat Carol with love and respect for all his days.

The attractive organist finished the soft music she was playing while people gathered and chatted. At the sound of the traditional "Wedding March" filling the sanctuary, all in attendance stood and turned to see Carol standing in the arched doorway, a vision of loveliness. Jonathan's heart overflowed with love for this woman—his dream come true.

Carol slowly glided toward him, discreetly waving to a few close friends in the pews. He could barely keep his emotions under control. He bit his lower lip and smiled as best he could under the circumstances until she was beside him. He reached for her hand she offered and placed it on his arm—his to have and to hold from this day forward as long as they both shall live.

EPILOGUE

With another Christmas approaching, so much has happened in Lucerne. Carol and Jonathan are happily married. Jonathan has proven to be an excellent partner to Carol in running Webster House. In addition, their pooled funds are purchasing more property where Jonathan will put his talents to work renovating while Carol tends to the decorating and business end of their partnership and the B&B.

As for Rob, he is still flying, still looking for the "perfect" woman to come along, although Heidi seems to be high on his list. He is helping Jim find a few more horses for the new riding ring under construction. He uses his Bonanza to travel to Kentucky breeding farms to check out gentle mares for sale. Jim will drive down in his new pickup with the trailer when choices are made that are gentle enough for neophyte riders. Perhaps Rob will come back to Lucerne when he retires.

Jim and Melissa are expecting the arrival of their first child next summer. She easily settled into Lucerne's way of life and was employed as a music teacher at the local school when the former teacher retired.

Michaela and Susan are both attending Penn State University at State College, coming back to Lucerne as often as possible.

Roberta will be married next summer at Webster House. Her job in Winchester was a good career choice. She and Duane will be spending Christmas with the Webster family this year.

Randall M. Block, esquire, accepted the honor of being a federal magistrate judge in Harrisburg, taking his faithful and devoted secretary Mamie with him. An article in the Westmoreland *Chronicle* noted their marriage November 15. They spend as much time as possible in the Lucerne home, maintaining a deep and lasting friendship with Carol and her new husband, in fact, with the Webster sons as well.

The romance between Martha and Tony is still developing but getting stronger all the time. Martha still lives in the garage apartment. She is a full-time employee doing the cleaning, laundry, cooking, and serving breakfasts. This gives Carol time to do the office work and help Jonathan in the design and decorating of houses they prepare for new arrivals to Lucerne to buy, bringing new blood into the recovering town. Ma's room has become the bridal suite with a four-poster canopied bed, as more and more weddings find the elegance of Webster House to be an ideal setting. Carol and Jonathan share her childhood room. A private balcony has been added.

The future looks great. As soon as Susie and Michaela finish their schooling, a much-needed veterinarian office will open in Lucerne.

There is no ending to this story—only new beginnings for the residents of this former coal-mining town.

ACKNOWLEDGMENTS

My thanks go, first of all, to Joy Duffy, my friend and instructor, who assigned the subject matter in a creative writing class. I did some research, made a few notes, sat down to my computer, and began writing. The characters I created came to life and took over. They didn't follow my notes at all.

I want to thank all my fellow members in WWOR, especially Ruth Miller; WOW, especially Colleen Shannon; members of Writer's Block; Shelley Kreider; family and longtime friends Jim and Edie McGough for supporting my writing habit, giving feedback, and encouragement.

Most of all, my eternal gratitude goes out to my dear husband for his patience when meals were late or for meals he made to allow me to keep writing.

ABOUT THE AUTHOR

Kay Black has had a lifelong love of writing, mostly family letters and short stories. As an avid reader and longtime member of two writing groups, honing her skills as a writer kept her busy and entertained as a hobby. Retirement gave her the free time to branch out and explore various genres. A creative writing class assigned coal as the subject of a short exercise. Her Pennsylvania coal-country roots gave her insight. The characters were developed; and this, her first fiction novel, was born.

A varied career life included raising two sons and a daughter, being a flight instructor, and owning several entrepreneurial businesses including a B&B inn. She and her husband now live near Knoxville, Tennessee, after living in nine different states and traveling extensively by RV. They share their home with three small dogs, two of them rescues.

CPSIA information can be obtained
at www.ICGtesting.com
Printed in the USA
JSHW020431210323
39228JS00001B/49